A Treasury of True Ghostly Humor

by L. B. Taylor, Jr.

Photographs by the Author
Illustrations by
Brenda Goens

Copyright © 2003 by L. B. Taylor, Jr.
Book Layout by InMind, Inc.
Printed in the U.S.A. by Progress Printing Co., Inc.

ISBN 1-928966-04-7

This book is gratefully dedicated to the hundreds of Virginians, from all across the commonwealth, who have, over the past 20+ years, generously shared their paranormal experiences with the author, and to the thousands of other Virginians who believe "some things cannot be explained."

Also, special thanks to Odette Seekamp of Williamsburg, who has, with great care, prepared this and many other manuscripts in this series.

Contents

Author's Note

In the past 20-plus years, in traveling all over the commonwealth, I have interviewed several hundred Virginians who have graciously shared their supernatural experiences with me. This has resulted in 14 previous books on the subject of Virginia ghosts – more than one million words and over 1,000 different encounters. All of this is part of our heritage.

In the process of endless hours of research – in the archives of libraries, on the internet, and in the backrooms of dusty old bookstores – I occasionally have discovered rare gems of haunting humor; priceless pearls of the paranormal that have wry, whimsical, and often hilarious twists.

I should note here that about half of these colorful anecdotes have been sprinkled throughout the 14 earlier books. But the other half – and there are more than 100 in the collection – are "fresh."

These amusing incidents do not, in almost all instances, directly involve confrontations with ghosts. Rather, they are about people's perceptions of what were thought to be ghosts. Fright often triggers the occurrences, which, when the real and rational source of the "manifestation" is revealed, frequently leads to light-hearted laughter. And the best part is they are all believed to be true accounts. Admittedly, some of them may have gotten embellished somewhat in the retelling from generation to generation. Nevertheless, they are all reported to be based on actual events. And in a 21st century world full of profane comedy, they provide a throwback to the times of good clean fun.

My goal is for readers to sample a pungent taste of Virginia's rich history regarding its customs, beliefs, traditions and legends – and, hopefully, to get a few hardy chuckles as well.

Enjoy!

THE DEAD SHALL RISE AGAIN!

century or more ago, one of the stark fears of Virginians was the horrific thought of being buried alive. It is said that Edgar Allan Poe was consumed with this terror. And in the days before embalming, and when medicine was far less sophisticated than it is today, such fears were sometimes justified. There are a number of cases on record where men and women, lapsed into deep comas, were pronounced dead, and, years later, when their coffins were opened for one reason or another, the gruesome discovery was made that they had awakened after being entombed six feet under.

In some instances, however, such "corpses" revived in time to be saved. Though undoubtedly shocking at the time, a few of these resurrections, in retrospect, were downright humorous. Here is a sampling.

The Grandmother Who Returned

Martinsville historian Carl DeHart tells of a bizarre event which occurred in 1938 on a dairy farm adjoining the famous Hairston plantation in Henry County. This estate was called Beaver Creek, and at one time stretched over several thousand acres.

A young black man named "Doc" Smith and his aged grandmother lived on the farm. She was described as wraith-like, with long white hair strung down her back. Youngsters in the area referred to her as "the ghost woman."

One day in mid-winter, when there were five inches of snow on the ground, Doc found his grandmother lifeless. He could discern no pulse or heartbeat. Because they were too poor to afford a coffin, he laid her out on a table in the main room of a two-room log cabin, and placed a bed sheet over her. As was the custom in those days, a "sitting up with the dead" session was held. Friends and relatives gathered to pay their last respects.

As it was freezing cold outside, a fire was going full blast in the fireplace and everyone was gathered around it, with their backs to the table. Suddenly, the sheet began to flutter. The warmth in the cabin had aroused the old woman from her catatonic deep sleep-like condition. She sat up, unnoticed by the mourners, slid off the end of the table, walked over to one of the men facing the fire, slapped him sharply on the back, and said, "Sho is cold out today, ain't it!"

Instant pandemonium! Hysterical screams echoed off the log walls, and there was a startled stampede to the front door. One man even tried to escape up the chimney!

******

A Premature Eulogy . . . and Sweet Revenge

The following is based on an interview held during the Works Progress Administration's writers' project in the late 1930s and early 1940s. The interviewee, on July 7, 1941, was Arch Mefford of Wise, Virginia.

"One day about 20 years ago, Lem Hall, well-knowed 'round Coeburn then, left to berry pick one day. Two fellows waylayed him and knocked him in the head and took his wad of money and left him for dead.

"But he came to long afterwards and got up and then made it to a house a little ways down the hillside. He got better and left the county right then, and everybody thought he had died out in the hills. They hunted all over for him but they never found him, and thought he'd fell in the water and washed down.

"Anyhow, they all thought he's daid, and some time later they's having a big meeting down in the meader and somebody spoke up and said a word or two that ought to be said about pore old Lem Hall. And then they got to talking about him right much. The preacher knowed him and started to talking right in the meeting there about him, and the first thing you knowed, they was all preaching , I don't know what all, about pore old Lem. I recollect they shouted and sung and preached about how awful it was to be called away from earth in that manner.

"Well, Lem, who had gotten himself a job over in Scott County, heard about all this. So the next day he got himself cleaned up and came home. When he was seen walking the streets of Coeburn, it like to have skeered everybody to death.

"The two fellows that had hit him in the haid and robbed him, lit out and haven't been heard of since!"

******

Buckshot Sawyer & the Lady in White

Joe White, a former sign painter from Glade Spring, used to regale listeners with humorous tales from the mountains and hollows of southwest Virginia. One of his favorites involved a man named Buckshot Sawyer. He worked, more than a half century ago, in an old quarry near Glade Spring, between Marion and Abingdon. His commute to work was so distant, he decided to live closer to the job, so he moved into an old shack at the edge of the mountains on the Bell farm.

"He put his bed in the shack," White said, "and one night he woke up and said there was this 'white lady' standing there. She had on a long white robe, and it glowed in the dark. Sawyer said she just looked down at him and said, 'Buckshot, nobody here but me and you tonight, is there?'

"And Buckshot replied, 'no maam, and as quick as I can get my britches on, ain't going to be anybody here but you'!"

******

The Man Who Had Two Funerals

Among the priceless gems of African-American ghost lore is this – an interview with Roscoe E. Lewis of Hampton, Virginia, recorded in the early 1940s.

"Dere was an ole man that use ta live here in Hampton that died twice, near as I can figure. His name was George Pleasants, and he lived somewhere on Lincoln Street. This happened way back yonder, 'bout 60 years ago, I reckon, 'cause ole man Pleasants was really buried here 'bout 15 years ago, and 'tween that time and de time of his first funeral, my wife and me got married and raised two children and they's got families of dere own now; so you see it musta been 'bout 40 years.

"Anyway, ole man Pleasants was a tall man, 'bout six feet tall, I reckon, and he had very broad shoulders. Musta weighted 'bout 200 pounds. He had a long flowing beard, 'twarn white and 'twarn black, so it musta been mixed, and he had long siders of de same texture. De ole man musta been a slave, I reckon, 'cause de first time he died, he died of ole age. Jes' went off in a trance for three days. The people felt awful bad 'cause he was dead. Cried and carried on like everything, they did.

"Laid him out on a board and called the undertaker. Undertaker Smith come rushin', befo' they'd git 'nother undertaker. Said he was dead alright, so he laid him out and shrouded him. Come back in a little while and eased him in a coffin.

"De funeral day was set and de mournful kinfolks come from everywhere. Funeral to be held at Queen Street Baptist Church. Ole undertaker Smith had two of de purtiest gray horses of 'airy a person in Hampton. They jes' a steppin' along, holdin' dere heads up high and everything, you know, like horses do. So they drive up to de church. Took ole man Pleasants' body in that church and preached his funeral. Yessir, Reverent Brown preached de funeral. Tole what a good man ole man Pleasants done bin, and preached him right on up to Heaven.

"They had de las' look, and everybody bust out cryin' when dey see him lyin' there so life like. Then de 'cession went on out and loaded up. All mourners started up Queen Street. They reached King Street and started to cross de cobbles, and that's where things happen, yessuh, right dare in front of de First Baptist Church.

"Ole man Pleasants woke up in de coffin and he heared de rumblin' of de hack wheels. Couldn' 'magine where he was. Got scared and started kickin' and a'scratchin' on de inside of de coffin. They heard all dis scufflin' and de undertaker opened de coffin. Ole man Pleasants, he always did talk real long and slow anyhow – he set up in his coffin right dere in de middle of King Street and yelled, 'Looky heah! Where you all goin'? Carry me back home. I ain't dead yet!'

"Mourners jes' bucked dere eyes and looked. They stood dere and stood dere, jes' couldn't understand. He didn't have to be daid 'cause de insurance warn't paid yet. Those days de paid off a few days after the funeral was over. So long as de money was all right, dey carried him on back home.

"Well, ole man Pleasants lived for many years after dat. I married and got grandchildren since den. Then he died de second time. They say he was sure 'nough daid de second time. Dey let him lay cold most nigh on to a week. . . Undertaker Smith's son, de man what is de undertaker now, had his body de second time. Had de second funeral at Queen Street Church, too. Church was packed.

"Everybody want to see if de ole man gonna git up again.

"This time Reverent Shorts preached it. Preached him back to Heaven again. De mourners was all on edge and it seem like de funeral couldn't git over quick 'nough. Undertaker clamped dat lid on dat coffin kinda quick like it seemed. Den dey started out to de graveyard again. When they gits to de First Church dis second time, everybody jes' a listening. Dey in cars dis time and all dey necks was craning.

"Ole man Pleasants ain't said nuttin' and he ain't done nuttin'. So dey went on to de graveyard 'bout a block further up. Slid dat rascal out right quick as de dirt was hittin' de coffin most soon as de preacher finished dat ashes to ashes resurrection stuff he says. Seem like everybody, mourners and all, was anxious to end dat piece of unfinished business.

"So, ole man Pleasants went on back home to rest de second time, and stayed. Leastways nobody ain't seen him since den; so he must be all right."

******

The Maple Tree that Revived a 'Dead' Woman

There is another account that is strikingly similar to the George Pleasants episode, as told by Dr. Jim Miller.

"There's this feller over in Pulaski County, his wife died. Had the undertaker come for her. They carried the body out the front door on a big board, across the porch, down the steps. And as they went across the yard, headed for the hearse, that board bumped against a maple tree in the yard.

"And the woman stirred! And they begun to work with her, and she revived up.

"That woman lived another ten years! Then she died again. And when the undertakers come for her this time, and started across the yard with her, her husband said, 'Uh, boys, watch out for that tree there'."

******

The Live 'Corpse' that Said 'Don't Shoot!'

The following account was taken from an old Roanoke newspaper item. Seems a crook running from the law concealed himself on an express train in 1886 by hiding in a coffin. The plan was to extricate himself from the pine box somewhere along the train's route and rob it.

But a railway agent, either alertly, or perhaps scared to death, foiled the attempt. He heard noise coming from the coffin. It is possible that he might have believed someone was coming back from the dead. Whatever, he piled some heavy freight on top of the casket, and when it arrived at the next station, the agent had it placed on the platform. He then yelled, "if anyone is in there, you'd better come out. I'm going to shoot through it."

A sheepish voice inside cried out, "I'm in here, don't shoot!" The chagrined would-be bandit was promptly arrested and subsequently received a three year prison term.

******

The Corpse that Sat Up

Sometimes the dead are really dead, but the appearance is otherwise. Such a case is related by Mary Daughdrill of Norfolk. According to Mary, her grandfather ran a sizeable farming operation in the early 1900s at what was known as the Bess Jarrell Plantation, despite suffering from a very severe physical handicap.

He was a hunchback, and his impediment was so great that he was nearly doubled over when he walked. He died sometime around 1915, and morticians had a difficult time fitting him into a casket. Mary says they had to strap him in to get the lid to shut. They placed his casket on the back of a wagon and headed to church for services. The road, however, was deeply rutted, and it was a jarring ride.

The church was packed, not only with friends, relatives and loved ones, but also with a large number of plantation servants who filled the back rows. At a point in the service, a gentleman went over to raise the lid of the coffin so everyone could get a final view of the dearly departed.

Unbeknownst to the brethren, however, the jolting ride to the church apparently had loosened or broken the straps holding the body down. So when the lid was raised, the body popped bolt upright, causing instantaneous panic in the church.

The building was, in fact, emptied within seconds!
******

A Frightening Eye Opener

Here is another instance where the deceased was thought to have returned from the beyond. It is told by Beverly Pace of Ridgeway, Virginia.

"One of my dad's first jobs back in the early 1950s was at the Mayberry Funeral Home in Floyd. He was a 'groomer,' that is he helped prepare the corpses for the families to view.

"One night he was alone working late to prepare a body which had to be ready by the first thing in the morning. As he stood above the man's head, he started to comb his hair straight back.

"When he did this, the corpse's eyes opened!

"Dad said he was so scared that he turned and ran from the funeral home as fast as his feet would carry him, the comb still in his hand. He would not go back in until the mortician arrived.

"What happened was that the mortician had forgotten to glue the eyes shut on the body, and when dad combed the hair straight back, it raised the man's eyelids!"

******

She Didn't Really Want Him Back

On the Eastern Shore, off Deal Island, there is a popular legend about a woman who got her wish – and then didn't want it. When her husband died, she had him buried in the island cemetery, but it was hard for her to let him go. It was said you could hear her crying late at night, saying, "Oh Lord, send him back to me!"

Several weeks later a hurricane swept through the Chesapeake Bay, flooding the island at high tide. The storm unearthed the coffin of the woman's husband and washed it up to her doorstep!

When she saw it out the window, she allegedly screamed, "Oh Lord, I don't want him. I didn't mean it. Take him back!"

******

Hallelujah, the Resurrection!

This anecdote, which occurred during Civil War times near the town of Middlebrook in Augusta County, was first published in the Staunton Spectator on April 7, 1886, and has been repeated down through the years, including a mention in folklorist-historian John Heatwole's interesting book, "Supernatural Tales."

In the years preceding, during, and immediately after the Civil War men of various ages, from teenagers to senior citizens, were called upon to serve in county militias in Virginia. Infrequently, during the year, they would be brought together for drills and for weapons' inspections. Such occasions, for some, became social events. Picnic lunches would be spread, and wives and children were invited. Families came from the hills and hollows all around to watch with pride their loved ones shoulder arms and march.

During these festivities one year, an elderly couple decided to leave early one morning before dawn for the walk to Middlebook, several miles away. As the sun began to rise amidst a heavy fog, they took a short cut through the St. John's Church cemetery. It so happened that another man heading toward the grounds passed by the graveyard at about the same time. When he looked over he was startled to see two bent over forms slowly moving through the tombstones, surrounded by the mist. He thought ghosts had arisen from the dead, and instinctively yelled out, "Go back, old man, go back! This isn't the general resurrection; it's only the Middlebrook muster!"

CHAPTER 2

A PORTFOLIO OF PHANTASMAL PRACTICAL JOKES

ince ancient times, inventive pranksters have used ghostly themes to perpetuate a variety of practical jokes – all aimed at scaring the pants off unsuspecting, and often superstitious victims. Mostly, such manufactured manifestations, many hatched around Halloween, result in uproarious laughter. But occasionally such gags, however well conceived, backfire. Here then is a selection of bizarre belly laughs.

A Voice from the Grave

This incident was authored by Works Progress Administration writer John W. Garrett, who interviewed Willie Agee in Alcoma, Virginia, on April 26, 1941:

"Willie Agee tells of a Negro funeral that took place one time, and there was very much grieving over the deceased, and as the funeral was to take place one afternoon, they had everything fixed up nice. They had a nice casket and he showed nice, but it was very hard to think about their loved one having to be put in the ground. They said we want the pall bearers to be the ones that was his real friends. They had lots of nice flowers, and was paying the last respects to him, and it came time for the funeral service. He was taken by the undertaker to the church and the parson gave a very impressive service.

"All of the family and pall bearers was very much touched

about the death of their loved one, and there was much weeping and shedding of tears, and the assertion was made that, 'oh, if I could only hear Paul speak again.' So the service was over at the church and the funeral procession was lined up and the pall bearers followed, and the family behind. Oh, it was a large crowd that followed to the family's burial ground.

"The casket was opened, and there was Paul lying all silent in death, ready to be put in the ground. And as the parson concluded the services at the grave, and the pall bearers looked on, and the family said, 'oh, if I could hear Paul speak again,' and the parson was reading the commital, and said 'ashes to ashes and dust to dust,' they let the casket drop a bit, and it was such grief to the people.

"So it was a fellow standing near by, that could throw his voice, and as the casket made the drop, the man spoke through Paul, and said, 'don't let me down so hard!'

"One of the pall bearers went back all excited and said to his boss, 'you know that Paul spoke out when he was let down in the grave a little, and said 'don't let me down so hard'.'

"'Well,' said the boss, 'what did the people do?'

"'I don't know,' replied the pall bearer. 'I warn't there'!"

******

A Second Voice from the Grave

Marvin D. Julian of East Stone Gap told the following to WPA writer James Taylor Adams during an interview on October 27, 1941"

"Here is a right funny thing that happened right up here in East Stone Gap cemetery. It's been three or four winters ago that Lee Qualls died up in the valley and they buried him here. About the time they got him put away, they come up an awful snow storm, so they just left the tent over his grave.

"One of his cousins from Scott County was going home the next morning and went by the cemetery to visit Lee's grave. It was before day when he got there, and another snow storm broke and he went in the tent and sat down.

"Worley Stidham, a young man up the valley, was on his way to work at the saw mill and he cut through the cemetery. He saw the tent there and sort of scrooched up against one side to shelter out of the snow storm. He was too timid to go in.

"The feller in the tent heard him run up to the tent and could see him pressed against the outside of the canvas. Being neighborly, he said, 'Bad weather out there.'

"The Stidham boy thought it was the dead man talking to him, and he liked to run hisself to death getting away from there, and swore that Lee Qualls (the dead man) spoke to him and asked him if it wasn't bad weather!"

******

Tricks and No Treats

(Author's note: I am indebted to my friend, 77-year-old Clara Gysbers of Seaford, Virginia, for the following two anecdotes she recalls from more than half a century ago.)

"Actually, this was in North Carolina," she says. "It was a small town and there was an elderly black preacher there who was said to be spellbinding. Whenever he held a revival meeting, blacks and whites attended in crowds, and this was in the days before integration in the South.

"Well, he always opened his revivals with the same prayer. 'Dear Lord, come down and be with us in our house of worship,' he would say. 'Please enter our building and our hearts.'

"Everyone knew this, so one time some high school boys decided to play a prank on the preacher. The night of one of the meetings, one of the boys – he was a football player about six foot five inches tall – he got a sheet and covered himself, and when the preacher asked the Lord to come visit, he burst through the church front doors and announced loudly, 'here I am!'

"They say such scrambling you've never seen before. People fell over people trying to get out of there as fast as they could, and some even jumped out the side windows."

******

The other instance Clara remembers involved a troop of faith healers who came into town. "To help draw attendance," she says, "they announced that they would walk on water. And they did! They walked right out several yards into the river. Some boys decided to check this out the next day. I don't know if they were the same boys or not, but they were just as mischievous.

"Anyway, they found that the faith healers had built some sort of little bridge just under the surface of the water, so that's how they walked on it. The boys went out into the river and took away the last section of the bridge. So that night when the faith healers traipsed out on the water, they got to a certain point and then they all got a good sound dunking. I guess you could say they got a baptism they didn't expect."

******

A Quick Cure for Lameness

This incident, related anonymously, occurred in Hanover County sometime early in the 20th century. It involved two old friends known only as John and Amos. John had been wheelchair-bound for about 15 years, and Amos often would take him places. John liked to visit a local cemetery, presumably to pay his respects to a departed friend or relative.

Some acquaintances of John and Amos knew of these frequent excursions and decided to play a Halloweenish-type trick. So one evening when Amos was pushing John towards the graveyard, the men hid in the bushes, and as the two passed, they leaped out at them, covered in white sheets.

Terrified at the ghastly sight, Amos immediately abandoned John in his chair and took off running as fast as his feet would carry him. He ran a good distance to a rural church, dashed up the stairs, entered the building and attempted to shut the door tight behind him. However, the door wouldn't shut. Something was holding it. Amos looked around and was astonished to see John right behind him.

"Don't close the door on me," John shouted.

The wheelchair was nowhere in sight!
******

A Most Dramatic Cure

Sam M. Hurst, author of "The Mountains Redeemed," a book about life in southwest Virginia during the early days, and published in 1929, tells a humorous story about two "Hardshell" Baptist apostles who had a fondness for moonshine liquor back in the 1920s. Nothing, it seemed, could discourage them from their regular binges; nothing, that is, until some sober-minded members of their congregation decided to scare the hell out of them – figuratively and literally.

So one night after both imbibers had passed into a drunken stupor, the members swung into action. They tied them up inside the skeleton of a long-deceased mule! When the two men awoke, they were staring directly into the bleached-white, grinning skull of the dead beast – a most frightening experience to say the least, especially, when, in their hung over condition, they became convinced they were face to face with "his Satanic majesty."

The ploy worked beyond expectations. Not only did they give up all forms of alcohol, but they also became the ministry's most outspoken advocates of abstinence!
******

The Talking Beast of the Mines

Here's another encounter involving a mule, specifically a dead mule. It was recorded by WPA writer James Taylor Adams who interviewed Leonard E. Carter of Glamorgan on February 2, 1941. Carter had heard about it 30 years earlier from a coal miner.

"I heard a feller at Glamorgan tell a tale one time about a haint-ed coal mine. He said it was at Pocahontas. One day, he said, two Negroes was loading coal when all at once a bony ol' mule trotted into their place. They thought it was a tram mule got loose from the driver, but they noticed it didn't have any gear on. That was strange but they didn't pay it any mind as all coal was hauled with mules then and the mines was full of them. You see, the coal is six to seven feet high at Pocahontas and they used big mules, not the little Santa Fe sort like they used to use 'round here.

"Well, sir, this feller, he said the Negroes jes worked on until the mule, it up and spoke, and says to them: 'You git yore tools together and get outen here!' And the Negroes didn't wait to argue with it. They got! They told everybody what they'd seed and heard, but people jes laughed at them. Nobody believed them. A mule couldn't talk.

"But the next day the mule walked into a room in the mines where two Hungarians was loading coal, and speaking in the Hungarian language, told them to git their tools and git out. And they got, too. They told what they seed and heard. Then people began to take notice. Funny, they thought, a talking mule would run two crews out of the mines.

"A lot of fellers boasted that they jes wished it would come in their place. Well, sir, nearly every time somebody got to boasting, it did visit them the next day. And the feller said the louder they boasted the faster they run. So it wasn't long till a lot of men was laying off, and the section in which most of the Negroes worked was closed down. They jes wouldn't go in the mines. Some miners would see a big rat run in their place and they'd walk right out and say they seed the talking mule.

"Things come to such a pass that one of the company men set himself up as a sort of detective to learn about the mule. He first went in the mine and all over it, but he couldn't find a hair nor hide of it. Then he went to the office and looked over the books. At last, he found that two Austrian coal loaders had been discharged about two months before and had soon left the boarding house where they'd been living.

"Then the feller set out again. A few days later he found the fired miners living in the old abandoned mine. They confessed that on the day they was fired that a mule had died and that gave them an idea to put the company out of business. They skinned the mule and dried its hide and used it to scare the miners with."

******

Shades of Ichabod Crane!

The following was recorded in 1941 by Works Progress Administration writer Lucille Jayne in Gloucester County, Virginia. In her preface she stated that "it is a story that has been handed down for over 100 years. It is a story of two prominent young men who were friends, sons of old Gloucester families, and their experiences in Old Ware Church, which at that time was not used, being partly in ruins. Anyone on horseback could ride right into the church, which many had done, when caught out in a storm."

Ware Church has been described as "a large rectangular structure, within a brick-walled enclosure, with steep gabled roof and walls three feet thick. Two large round arched windows light the

chancel and five others are in the side walls. The church, built about 1700, has a door in both north and south walls. Before the chancel, but now covered by flooring, are table tombs."
(These tombs were still visible when this incident occurred.)

Writer Jayne described one of the young men as "dashing, very bold and proud, one who boasted of his courage . . . fear he did not know . . . and nothing could make him as much as flinch because of fear." The other youth was "jolly" and loved a practical joke.

"It happened one stormy night in June, when the rain from the skies did pour, the thunder crashed, and the night was black, except when illumined by the lightning flashing through the sky. These two youths were out pleasure seeking, but each in a different direction."

Each was caught in the storm but was unaware that the other was also out. The carefree young man came upon Ware Church first. "The church had rather a spooky look, especially when the lightening flashed, revealing all the tombstones, making it look kind of ghostly. So he rode on in" on his pale white horse. Since he had never boasted of having no fear, he admitted he felt "a little might shaky." He reined in his mount close to the wall, "and there he sat trembling in spite of himself.

"Soon up rode the boastful youth that 'knew no fear.' mounted on a nettlesome horse as black as the night. He was trembling and shaking, though even to himself he was too proud to admit he was afraid.

"The other youth, seeing him as he rode in, thought to himself, 'Now time will soon tell whether, as you boast, you have no fear.' So he sat perfectly quiet on his white horse, which must have been rather a ghostly looking sight.

"The newcomer felt his boasted courage fleeing, and fear so terrible replacing it when he finds himself alone as he supposes in an old deserted church among the dead at midnight, while the thunder crashes and the wind does blow. . . He did not feel just right alone among the dead at this hour of the night.

". . . A flash of lightening illumines the opposite wall of the church, and there he sees a sight that fairly freezes his blood and makes his hair stand up; a horse ghostly white with a motionless rider. . . He cried, 'What art thou? Speak!' For reply, he hears only a hollow groan.

". . . Overcome with fear, he cries 'Enough,' and furiously spurring his horse in frantic haste, he goes, only to find coming swiftly on his track, the 'ghost,' with speed fully equal to his own. Now thoroughly frightened, he cries, 'Good steed, now do your very best or I'll surely be lost!'

"Quickly, the miles fly by, still he urges his faithful steed, till at last he sees his home right at hand, and as he madly dashes through the gate, he turns to see the 'ghost' still mounted on the white horse pass swiftly by.

"Then, to his astonishment, he hears a jeering laugh he recognized as his neighbor's, who then cries out, 'Ha! My brave friend, I see indeed that fear you know not . . . at least not till you perchance do meet a ghost in the Old Ware Church'."

Realizing he had been tricked, "and thus displayed such cowardly fear at only a man mounted on a pale horse in a deserted church," he now was afraid he would never hear the end of it. And if the story got out, and he was certain it would, knowing his friend's reputation as a practical joker, he would soon be the joke of the community. He couldn't stand this.

So he concocted a plan. He invited his friend over for a lavish dinner the next day. He then elicited from his friend the fact that he had not yet told anyone about the episode the previous night.

He then drew a pistol on his friend and said, "'you hold a secret that to me is dearer than life. You saw me in Old Ware Church yield to cowardly fear, and if you value your life very highly and are not over anxious to die, you will gladly promise this secret to keep and guard it most carefully as long as I live. And if by chance you should outlive me, you are welcome to tell the whole, for I know your love for a practical joke'."

His friend, at gunpoint, instantly replied, "'I solemnly promise never to tell the tale as long as you live, but if I should outlive you, why then I can't promise in that event, for it is too good a story to be lost'."

The two friends then drank to each other's health.

The oath that was sworn was faithfully kept for many years – that is, until the "fearless" young man died first.

******

Another Four Legged 'Ghost'

From the book, "John Jay Janney's Virginia – an American Farm Lad's Life in the Early 19th Century," one can gain an unusual insight into what life was like in the commonwealth in the 1800s. Following is an incident which occurred when Janney was a youth:

"Some localities were believed to be haunted. There was a deep, heavily-timbered ravine just on the east line of my grandfather's farm, which the 'big road' crossed. Many of the neighbors were afraid to cross it on a dark night, and it was known through the neighborhood as the 'haunted hollow.' We never learned the origin of the title, and never heard of but one ghost in it.

"There was a grog shop half a mile beyond it, at which some of the farm hands would gather on Saturday evenings. Joe McGeth, who worked for my grandfather, was one of them and he would sometimes get quite tipsy. He had a little dog which followed him everywhere, and one evening when Joe had become quite drunk, the boys caught his dog and tied all the white rags they could find around him, so that he looked like a big bundle of rags.

"Just as Joe reached the edge of the hollow, he heard something behind him, and looking back, saw his dog. With a wild 'hellow,' he broke into his best gait and kept up his yelling. The folks in the kitchen heard him coming. He came with a yell, tramping on the porch, and as they opened the door, Joe fell headlong on the floor. Just as they raised him to his feet, his dog came panting in, and then the shouts of laughter brought Joe to his senses. That was the only ghost ever really seen or heard in the hollow."

******

The Fire Plug 'Ghost'

This was extracted from the August 5, 1898 edition of the Alexandria Gazette:

"Some practical jokers on Wednesday night clothed the fire plug on Christ Church corner on Washington Street in white for the purpose of making it look like a ghost. The perpetrators of the joke then secreted themselves for the purpose of witnessing the effect it would produce on certain individuals who would pass that way on their return home from an entertainment in the northern part of the city.

"The parties expected soon afterwards came along, and the antics of some of the belated individuals are said to have been amusing. A number of the party espied the object half a square away and took care to cross to the opposite side of the street. Others came close upon the plug before they noticed it, and went out into the street, passing around the supposed spook and at a convenient distance from it. None, it is said, had sufficient nerve to come in close enough proximity to examine the object, and most of those who saw it had blood-curdling stories to relate when they reached their homes."

******

Not Yet Ready to Cross Over

This anecdote was gleaned from the April 1903 issue of the Confederate Veteran Magazine. It involves an aged slave known as Uncle Abram. The exact location and date of the incident were not recorded, although it is likely it occurred on a rural Virginia

plantation in the years before the Civil War.

"Uncle Abram, who was inclined to look on Jordan as a hard road to travel, sat alone by his cabin fire at the close of a winter day and poured out his lamentations with intense audibility:
'O Lord, Uncle Abe am mighty tired and 'stracted. O Lord, please, Massa, send de angel Gabriel to take ole Uncle Abe up to heben, cause he sho' don't want to lib no mo'.'

"Uncle Abe's employer, just returning from a fox hunt and passing the cabin, was attracted by the dismal monologue, and paused to hear the nature of the old man's complaint. Knowing the direct association in the mind of the Negro of a trumpet and the angel Gabriel, the huntsman placed his horn close to the latch-string, and its blast startled the old Negro to his feet.

"'Who dat at dat do?' he nervously asked. 'It's the angel Gabriel come to take old Uncle Abram up to heaven,' a sonorous voice replied.

"'Massa, Massa Gabriel, old Uncle Abe don't lib here!'"

******

The Siren in the Cemetery

Story teller Joe White of Glade Spring often told about the time when he was a teenager in Saltville and ran around with "a bunch of devilish mean boys." "They kept saying there was this little old graveyard over there at an old quarry, and that they'd see things there passing by you. They'd see something white just raise up out of the ground and stand.

"So they's having a revival down at the church one night, and one of the boys got a little siren off of a bicycle. This one was turned by a crank. There were four or five of us, and we got in the graveyard, and when the church let out and the crowd come by yonder, we started that siren . . . wwhhirr . . . real low, you know. They all stopped and listened. And then we cranked it up a little louder, and those people took off and ran in all directions!"

******

A Scary Moment at Rosewell

There are hauntings enough at the ruins of Rosewell, the once-magnificent 18th century plantation home of the Mann Page family in Gloucester County, which was gutted by fire in 1916. One does not have to make up manifestations here, but such, apparently, was the case a few years ago, as recorded in Claude Lanciano, Jr's. fine book, "Rosewell, Garland of Virginia."

Seems a group of tourists were on their way to visit the ruins one day. A Colonial Williamsburg employee named Joe Nicolson was on his way home in Gloucester County, and decided to stop by Rosewell to take some photos. He was still dressed in his colonial costume, complete with buckled shoes to ruffled collar. It should be added that Joe is a gaunt, spare man, 110 pounds and

Rosewell

19

five feet nine inches tall. Lanciano wrote that Joe had "a facial aspect that might be described as half-way between somber and cadaverous."

Anyway, Joe was milling about in the ruins when he heard the tourist group arrive, chattering away. He decided to have some fun. As the tourists lined up facing the ruins, he suddenly sprang up from out of the shadows behind a still-standing chimney, and announced, "Good evening ladies and gentlemen. I'm Governor Page!"

The response was a stunned silence. The tourists froze in their tracks, and two ladies nearly fainted.

******

More than He Expected

Chuck Ferebee of Yorktown, a Civil War reenactor, says several of his fellow participants have told him of feeling "strong presences" at battlefield sites. A few years ago, Chuck adds, some of his buddies decided to play a practical joke. This time it worked in reverse.

"One of the guys laid down on the ground and was buried in a pile of leaves at a small cemetery," Chuck recalls. "The idea was that when someone walked by, he was going to rise up out of the leaves and scare them.

"But before anything could happen, the guy who was buried started screaming, leaped up, and ran toward us. He was three shades of white and obviously terrified.

"He said while he was laying under the leaves, something 'cold' reached up and touched his face!"

******

Scared in Reverse

A young man from the southwestern part of the state, who preferred to remain anonymous, once told of the time, many years ago, when he and a friend decided to play an unkind joke on two girls. Seems they had already frightened them with tales of a headless man who roamed the woods behind their house.

So when night fell, they asked the girls to fetch some fresh water down at the springs, which was a couple of hundred yards away, bordering on the edge of the woods. Reluctantly, the girls went. Unbeknownst to them, the two young men, carrying a white bed sheet, took a short cut, and beat them to the springs.

When the girls had half filled their jugs, the men sprang out from the darkness covered by the sheet. But their expectations of scaring the girls went far beyond their imagination.

Instead of screaming and running off, as anticipated, both girls collapsed to the ground in dead faints.

Now it was the young men who were scared. It took some time for them to revive the girls, and they vowed never to play such a trick again.

******

The Non-Ghost Who Became a Corpse

Talk about a practical joke backfiring – this must be the ultimate case. In his fine book, "Home to the Cockade City, the Partial Biography of a Southern Town," published more than a half century ago, author M. Clifford Harrison tells of a most extraordinary murder case that occurred in Petersburg, probably some time late in the 19th century. It had been told to him by his grandfather.

It seems, at that time, there was a shoemaker who somehow had gained a reputation among the townspeople as being totally fearless. It was said that he had never been scared in his life. Apparently, some young men, with mischievous intentions, decided to put the cobbler's courage to the test.

He was told that a certain house was haunted, and that a person had recently died there, but because of the threat of ghosts, no one would "sit up with the dead." It was the custom then for someone to sit up all night in the parlor where the recently departed lay in a coffin. The shoemaker accepted the challenge. He would sit up with the dead by himself.

He took some tools of his trade with him so he could repair some shoes during the nocturnal vigil. As Harrison wrote: "An open coffin stood in the middle of a bleak room. Outside, the wind wailed. Eerie creaks and groans sounded through the lonesome building. The shoemaker unceremoniously drew up a chair and went to work."

At about midnight, a strange thing happened. Silently, the "corpse" began to rise, "until it was sitting up in the coffin." Instead of being frightened out of his wits, the shoemaker looked at the scary phenomenon and commanded, "Lie down!" The "body" laid down. An hour or so later, the same thing occurred. The body rose. This time, the cobbler shouted, "Lie down and say down, and I'm not going to tell you again!" The order was again obeyed. At about two a.m., the body arose a third time. The shoemaker, without a word, took his hammer and cracked the skull of the "corpse's" head! As Harrison concluded: "This time the practical joker in the coffin – whose friends had powdered him up to make him look cadaverous – was a corpse sure enough."

******

21

Another Most Tragic 'Joke'

The following account is more ironic than funny; a scary prank for which the perpetrator paid the supreme price. It was recorded by Works Progress Administration writer James Taylor Adams, who interviewed the Reverend John A. Robbins in Big Laurel, Virginia, on August 30, 1941.

"One time two men went into a new county and took up land right side by side. Great big boundaries. Went on and one of the men died. His widow and children decided to jes stay on and make the best of it.

"The other feller got to thinking that he'd like to have both places. He tried to buy the widow out by offering some little sum for her place. She wouldn't sell. So he planned out how he'd make her sell.

"He killed an owl and that gave him an idea. He took the owl's claws and went up close to her house one night and squealed like a panther. The screaming come right on up closer and closer. She barred the doors.

"There was a big tree stood by the house. After while they hear something climbing the tree, then 'ker-thump' it struck the

roof and began clawing and scratching with them owl claws, jes like it was going to tear the boards off.

"The woman grabbed her husband's old rifle gun and stuck it up through the loft and fired. She heard something going rolling and tumbling and strike the ground in the yard. She wuz afraid to open the door.

"But the next morning she opened the door and there laid her neighbor, dead and stiff!"

******

How to Get Rid of a Mother-in-Law

In his entertaining book, "Pioneers in Paradise," author V. N. (Bud) Phillips tells hundreds of marvelous true anecdotes about the city of Bristol, including 100 pages of ghost lore. The following hilarious account is excerpted from that collection, with permission.

Phillips wrote of a house that bordered on the East Hill Cemetery. The date isn't cited, but it was back in the days when "outside plumbing" was still used. The backside of this particular outhouse was only a few inches from a monument marking a grave.

One day a young couple from Abingdon moved into the house, and everything went well for the husband, except when his mother-in-law came to visit. She was described as a "rather obese and lazy woman, was querulous and nitpicking, and daily giving an abundance of unsolicited and unappreciated advice."

Though she constantly complained about the house – that it was too close to what she called "that scary old graveyard" – she came often to visit her daughter, and "stayed long." Her bedroom faced the cemetery, now largely overgrown with weeds and bushes, and she was terrified of what she called "hants."

It was her habit to retire each evening promptly at nine o'clock, and just before going to bed, she would traipse out to the outhouse. She knew about the sunken grave just in the back of it, and each night as she walked across the yard, she would sing an old ballad, in an apparent attempt to "drown out any ghostly sounds that might arise from the cemetery." Her son-in-law even thought she made the trip with her eyes closed, since she seemed to stagger on the way.

It eventually dawned on the young man that perhaps he could use the old woman's fear to his advantage in getting her to shorten her stay at the house. He conceived a devious plan. He got a neighbor's boy to sneak out behind the outhouse one night. Precisely at nine, he heard the woman singing, then she closed the door and sat down. Suddenly, there was a sharp rapping on the back of the outhouse, then a loud moan that turned into a wail.

The woman stopped singing and shrieked, "Lordy, what wuz that?" Then came a quivering ghostly voice: "I'm coming in to get you!"

In stark terror, the woman shot up from her seat and didn't even bother to unlatch the door. She crashed into it, knocking it off its hinges onto the ground outside. Because she hadn't even stopped to pull up her under britches, she leaped over the fallen door like a frog trying to escape from a snake, then she hip-hopped smack into the middle of a thorny rosebush. Undaunted by the scratches, she pogo-jumped all the way up onto the porch, through the back door of the house, then slammed it shut and locked. it.

Inside, she ran to her room, packed her bags and announced she was going to take the late train home to Abingdon. Her obliging son-in-law, biting the tip of his tongue not to laugh, escorted her to the depot on time.

There, she dramatically declared that she would not return to that dreadful place until they moved. They did, years later, after the mother-in-law had passed on.

******

A 'Hant Healing'

Here's another jewel from Bud Phillips' Bristol book, "Pioneers in Paradise." During the 1860s, a band of bushwhackers raided an antebellum house on Washington Street and shot the owner. As he lay dying, his blood ran through cracks in between the floorboards and formed a dark pool on the living room floor below. The large stain could be seen there as long as the house stood.

A few years later the man's widow sold the house, and the new family soon after reported strange happenings. They heard unexplained sounds of someone groaning and loud, labored breathing. Occasionally, a gunshot would seem to go off in the loft, where the murdered man had hidden when he was accosted. And there were unaccountable footsteps in the loft, plus rappings on the walls. The most frightening sound was a resounding thud, as if a body had plummeted to the floor, followed by what appeared to be blood dripping through cracks in the loft flooring. The word spread through the town: the house was haunted!

Some time later, the father of the family living in the house became desperately ill. It appeared that he soon might die. As was the custom in those days, neighbors came over to sit up with him through the night.

It happens that one of the sick man's sons had a penchant for practical jokes. Knowing of the house's reputation for ghostly sights and sounds, he decided to play a prank on those present for the nightly gatherings. So one morning he carried a jar of pokeberry juice up into the loft, along with something to recreate the sound of a body thumping downward. He then rigged strings and dropped a pull cord through a hole in the floor to a dark corner of the room below.

That evening, the neighbors congregated as usual. The son then regaled the group by telling them of all the haunting noises that the family had experienced. When everyone seemed appropriately taut with nervousness, and weren't looking at him, he jerked the cord. There was a sudden thud in the loft, and then a flood of "blood" came pouring through the cracks in the ceiling.

Author Phillips described what happened next: "Those people sprang up, gasping, screaming, and yelling, all bent on sailing out the windows or the door, whichever was closer." And guess who was the first through the front door? The supposedly mortally ill father, leaped up from his sick bed, and, with sheets and covers still tangled around him, made it to the door in no more than two leaps and was gone.

Phillips said the man miraculously recovered from his illness and lived for another 15 years.

A MEDLEY OF MISCELLA-NEOUS 'MANIFESTATIONS'

Some hauntingly humorous incidents are difficult to classify or catagorize; they don't fit any set theme. Here are some examples:

Painting an Apparition Black

On August 6, 1767, the Virginia Gazette, printed in Williamsburg, published the following letter describing a most bizarre encounter with the supernatural.

Seems a gentleman of means, newly married, was awakened late one stormy night by his bride, who said she thought there was a ghost in the room. He "was so terrified that he immediately jumped out of bed, and knowing there was a bottle of holy water in a closet in the room, he walked over to take it out, without any more light than that of the constant lightning, and soon began to sprinkle his Lady, himself, and even the furniture to engage, without doubt, the protection of Providence.

" . . . He returned to bed pretty well composed, and began to value himself highly on the efficacy of his operation; but how great was his surprise when, at daylight, he awoke and turned toward his Lady, who he found as black as a curlpated inhabitant of Africa, and all the bedding, tapestry and furniture of the room of the same melancholy complexion."

What had happened? In the darkness the night before, as he reached for the holy water, he instead snatched up a bottle of ink!

******

From a Disenchanted Husband

Here's another item from the Virginia Gazette, a poem published on March 16, 1738. It was obviously from a woman hater.

"If all the Plaques beneath the Sun,
To love's the greatest Curse;
If one's deny'd then he's undone
If not, 'tis ten times worse.
Lovers the Strangest Fools are made,
When they their Nymphs pursue;
Which they will ne'er believe 'til Wed,
But then they find it true.
They beg, they pray, and they implore,
Til wearied out of Life;
And pray what's all this trouble for?
Why truly for a Wife.
Each Maid's an Angel while she's woo'd,
But when the Wooing's done,
The Wife, instead of Flesh and Blood,
Proves nothing but a Bone."

******

It Must Be Hell

One of the author's favorite letters was from a lady in Philadelphia who wrote that she and her husband had been marred for 26 and a half years.

******

The Screaming Non-Ghost in the Oak Tree

One of the zaniest incidents recorded in Richard Edward Beaty's book, "The Blue Ridge Boys," tells of a Civil War deserter who found himself imprisoned, not by the Confederate Army from which he ran, but by Mother Nature!

When the south began drafting eligible young men for military service, in 1861, one of the first to be tapped was the older brother of a young man named Bill Plunker, who lived in the heart of the Shenandoah Valley. The problem was, Bill's brother was too sick to report. So Bill went as his replacement.

After two years of faithful service, Bill was granted a 30 day furlough. While at home, his brother passed away. This caused a dilemma. Did that mean Bill didn't have to return to the war, since his brother was the one who had been drafted, and now he was

dead? Bill went to a regional commander and put the question to him. He was told, bluntly, and without due consideration, to report back immediately to his unit.

This rubbed Bill the wrong way, and he decided to desert. He hid out in the mountain forests of the Blue Ridge for the last two years of the war. One of his favorite hiding places was in the top of a large oak tree which had a hollow place high up where he could stand and survey the countryside for miles around. It was a perfect natural look out station.

But one day as the end of the fighting neared, while Bill was standing high in the tree, the rotting wood beneath his feet gave way, and he crashed down to the earth about 25 feet below, now totally encased by the towering oak. He tried desperately to climb out, to no avail. He clawed at the ground trying to dig out, but that, too, proved futile.

Frantically, he began screaming at the top of his lungs, hoping someone passing by might hear him. This in itself likely would have driven any witnesses away, thinking the tree was haunted. But finally, after spending three or four days so entombed, a friend out hunting happened to hear Bill's cries and recognized his voice. A "doorway" was chopped into the oak's base, and an emaciated and much-chagrined Bill Plunker was rescued from his natural "prison."

******

The Ghost that Smoked

Ghosts can be nuisances at times, according to Amy Barnwell of Springfield, Virginia. Amy says one stole her cigarettes!

Some time ago she was staying at a friend's house in Winchester. It was built in the early 1800s, and Amy says "there are some creepy things going on inside." Outside is a still standing slaves' quarters and a small family cemetery with two visible tombstones. It is believed Civil War fighting took place on the front lawn, which still has the signs of trenches.

Amy says one night she put her pack of cigarettes on the night stand beside her bed and fell asleep. "The next morning I woke up, reached for my cigarettes, and they were gone! Thinking that maybe I had somehow knocked them on the floor, I checked but they weren't there. When I got up and dressed, I noticed the room was freezing cold."

Amy adds that she found the pack of cigarettes on a table in front of a couch – on the other side of the room – and the pack was empty!

******

President Who?

This is not a ghostly legend, but it is, nevertheless a gem that occurred in the early days of the American Civil War. And it indicates how totally isolated and ill-informed some of the residents in the far mountainous reaches of western Virginia were in those days. It was taken from an old, out of print book and reprinted in the booklet, "Stories, Anecdotes and Humor from the Civil War," collected by Hugh and Judy Gowen.

Seems a Union soldier came upon a crude cabin in a hollow miles from any neighbors. Out came a wrinkled old woman well into her eighties. They talked for awhile and as the soldier prepared to depart, he said, "you'll not refuse to hurrah for Old Abe, will you old lady?"

Puzzled, the woman said, "Who's Old Abe?"

"Why Abraham Lincoln, President of the United States," the soldier answered.

The woman got a funny look on her face and responded, "Why, hain't General Washington President?"

"No," she was told. "he's been dead for more than 60 years."

Dumbfounded, the woman hollered into the cabin, "Hey, son, come here a minute." Out ambled a bearded man of about 50. "What is it, Maw?" he asked.

"Would you believe it, son," she exclaimed. "General Washington's dead. Sakes alive! I wonder what's going to happen next."

******

How a Slave Got His Pig

The following is excerpted from an old Virginia family history written in 1910. The event described likely happened in the antebellum days preceding the Civil War.

There was, at the time, a wealthy plantation owner. He had a number of pigs. One of his slaves loved pork, and contrived a plan to steal one of the pigs. He killed one and hid it in the family cemetery. He planned to go back at night and retrieve it. But he

quickly had to improvise when a neighbor came over to view a new tombstone that had just been placed in the graveyard. Upon seeing the slain swine, she immediately went to the master to inform him.

After dinner, Judge Frank Christian, the proprietor, and his son, Johnny, walked out to the cemetery to try and solve the puzzle. But they saw no pig. Instead, there was a loud, mournful yell. Johnny asked his father what it was. He was told it probably was an owl. As they neared the graves, there was a second and more loud and distinct groan. This was no owl! And then, amidst the tombs, there came a third "deafening and agonizing cry" from the very site of the new headstone.

It "struck a resistless terror to Johnny's heart and, answering it with a cry almost as painful, he took to his heels and soon found himself (in spite of darkness and obstructions), safe in his father's home! And the painful truth was that Judge Christian was only a little way behind his son in the race homeward."

And so, the slave had his pig.

******

An Odious Ouija Experience

Ouija boards can be fun. But to some a session on the "Witch board" can be a frightening experience. To many, Ouija is just a game, but others contend it is a true method of communicating with spirits from the beyond.

Here, however, is an instance where a Ouija participant thought he was being haunted by such a spirit, only to find out, to his equal displeasure, that the source of his fear was quite earthy.

It happened a few years ago to a chagrined teenager from eastern Maryland who shall remain nameless to avoid any future embarrassment.

A friend of his owned an Ouija board. He had always heard that if you burn such a board, you will hear "horrible screams." (One of the many superstitious beliefs associated with the game.) He took this as a "dare," and decided to see if the legend had any truth to it.

So one evening he took his friend's set, soaked it with an entire can of lighter fluid, and set it ablaze in his backyard grill. The board was quickly engulfed in flames.

"What happened next," he said later, "will continue to haunt me forever. I found out what the curse of the Ouija board was."

Expectantly, he waited for the screams to shrill through the neighborhood, but there were none.

Then, suddenly, he said he was "overwhelmed by a terrible odor." Was this an evil sign from the other world?

Well, no. He looked down at his feet, and in the darkness, he had stepped squarely into a large pile of . . . dog poop!

******

The Man Who Outran a Streetcar

In her 1932 classic book, "Virginia Ghosts and Others," author Margaret DuPont Lee tells of a startling, yet amusing incident that happened to a well known Washington, D. C. physician. While the date is not recorded, it probably happened sometime in the late 1800s. A good friend of the doctor's had just died and he paid a visit to comfort the man's widow.

Afterwards, on the way home, he boarded a street car. He gave the conductor a quarter, which, at the time, yielded six tickets. When he got on there was only one other passenger, an African American.

Curiously, the conductor detached two tickets instead of one. When the doctor asked why, the conductor said, "for you and the gentleman who came in with you." The doctor protested that no one had accompanied him, but the conductor insisted, "Yes, he did; he is sitting beside you!" The doctor then asked for a description of the phantom passenger, and the conductor perfectly described his friend, who had just passed away! "Why that man is dead," the doctor exclaimed.

At this, the African-American leaped to his feet and shouted, "My God! If dat dere man I sees sittin' on dat seat am daid, let me git off dis heah car!" He jerked the bell and soon was lost to sight!

******

A Witness from the Beyond

In "Legends of Virginia Courthouses," published in 1933, author John H. Gwathmey recounts a humorous event involving attorney C. A. Branch of Williamsburg, and his "star witness," a black man named Elijah White. It was the early 1900s, and it seems the two men's paths crossed a number of times, mostly when Branch was defending White from a variety of charges ranging from disorderly conduct to assault with "intent to mayhem."

Some said it was not so much Branch's lawyering, but more

the guile and shrewdness of White that allowed the defendant to invariably escape conviction, even though, as author Gwathmey noted, "he was constantly getting into trouble of one kind or another." In fact, White was acquitted so many times one judge remarked there was no use arresting him anymore. He was so cunning that Branch not infrequently called upon White as a witness in other trials.

Some years later Branch passed away, and "not very long afterward," Elijah was struck and killed by a railroad train. Within a day or two a citizen of Williamsburg stopped by one day at Captain Bob Timberlake's store and relayed the news. Captain Bob had known both Branch and White well and had been either a witness or a juror at some of White's trials.

When he was told of White's accident, he proclaimed: "Fo Gawd, Mr. Branch has got in trouble and sent for his star witness!"

******

Another Mother-in-Law Story

Folklorian collector Elmer Smith of Harrisonburg relates a death wish that ended on a note of wry humor. A dying woman asked her husband for one last favor before she passed on – for him to let her mother ride with him to her funeral. Without hesitation, he replied, "Why can't she leave earlier. Then she could go with you!"

******

How to Chase Ghosts Away

In the annals of African-American folklore there is this gem: There was an empty house in a rural area that had long had a reputation for being haunted. No one would stay in it for any length of time, and it eventually was abandoned altogether. The phenomena involved inexplicable sounds – moans, phantom footsteps, and rattling chains.

So one evening a circuit-riding preacher came to the area and asked about for a night's lodging. He was told about the haunted house, but said he had no fear of the unseen, and calmly entered the place, alone. As it was getting late, he lit a candle, went upstairs to a bedroom, took out his Bible, and started reading. The fearsome noises began. Unperturbed, he announced that he was going to stay in the house all night. He started preaching and praying aloud. The rattling and rumbling sounds continued.

Finally, the preacher felt enough was enough. He took off his hat, used it as a collection plate, and walked all around the room, from wall to wall. He said the noises immediately ceased, and he lapsed into a sound a restful sleep!

******

She Wasn't Ready to Go Yet

The following was recorded by WPA writer Gertrude Blair, who interviewed "Minnie the cook," June 9, 1939, in Roanoke:

"While I was in the kitchen of the home where I live, the other day Minnie (the cook) was in a talkative mood. She told several stories of 'hants' coming in her room; and of a recent visit by her husband, who died several years ago. . . There is no power that would ever shake her belief in 'hants.'

"Well, she said that before the Yale lock was put on her door, her husband paid her a visit in the dead hours of the night. When she awoke, he was standing by her bed, looking down at her. Minnie said 'he looked just as 'natrall.'

"I said, 'Why Minnie, didn't it scare you to death?'

"'No, I jes say Jim, for God's sake, what is you doin' here? He says, Minnie, I'se come for you.'

"'I told him when the Lord's ready for me, He'll come. He won't send you. I ain't seen him since'."

******

A Helpful Reference Source

(Author's note: In doing research for my regional book "The Ghosts of Tidewater," (1990), I talked to a young lady in Gloucester who, in trying to be helpful, told me that her mother had a "marvelous" book all about ghosts and that if I could locate a copy in the library she was sure I would find everything I was looking for. She would ask her mother what the title was and get back to me. The next day she called and said the book was "The Ghosts of Richmond," and the author was L. B. Taylor, Jr. We both had a hearty laugh over that when she realized who I was.)

******

The Cat that Talked

Michael Renegar of East Bend, North Carolina, says he has a friend who once lived in Ridgeway (south of Martinsville near the

Carolina line, and just west of Danville). She told him that "they had a cat that could actually talk!" Whenever it would get shut into the bathroom, they'd hear a voice distinctly calling, 'Let me out! Let me out!' It would also say things like 'hello' and 'good-bye.' Michael added that he believed her because she wasn't the type to "pull his leg."

******

The Curious Funeral Of Billy Gilliam

A long-standing legend in Williamsburg concerns the unusual funeral of a man named Billy Gilliam, sometime shortly after the Civil War.

Billy was still a young man when he died of unspecified causes. Like many others in town, he had been a member of the "Wise Light Infantry," a group of military volunteers who had organized under the leadership of a Dr. Wise, then a professor at the College of William and Mary. So it was decided to give Billy a military funeral.

When members of the unit arrived at his house, they found Billy laid out in his casket in his full Wise Light Infantry uniform. This seemed to cause a problem, since the group had not yet paid for the uniforms. A quick meeting was held and it was decided to strip the body of the coat, which could be used by another member.

What happened next is somewhat shrouded in mystery. The detail of young men started up the street with the coffin as their little band played "Hop Light, Ladies, the Cake's All Dough."

It wasn't exactly a tune designed for the occasion, but the band only knew two numbers, "Hop Light" and "Dixie."

Up Duke of Gloucester Street they went, headed for the cemetery, when all of a sudden a young boy rushed up to the procession and stopped it. He was out of breath and stammering, and there was some confusion.

Finally, he got his message out. Somehow, back at Billy's house, when his coat was taken off, his body was never placed back in the coffin. He was left at home!

So the Wise Light Infantry turned around, marched back to the house, placed Billy in the coffin, and headed back up the street, still marching to "Hop Light Ladies."

After the service at the cemetery, Captain Wise ordered a volley to be fired over the grave. But there was another slip up. The men mistakenly had been issued live cartridges instead of the usual blanks. One of the stray shots killed a cow in a nearby pasture.

The unit was compelled to pay for the cow, which depleted the infantry's treasury and led to its financial ruin and subsequent disbandment.

******

The Body that Disintegrated

Talk about shock! Joseph B. Yount, III, a Waynesboro attorney, tells the following about a most frightening incident which occurred at an ancestral home, Stonewall Cottage, in Rockingham County, just north of Harrisonburg.

In 1938, several family graves were to be moved from the land at Stonewall Cottage to lots in Woodbine Cemetery at Harrisonburg. Among those to be transferred was that of Captain Joseph M. Dovel.

Says Yount: "He was a young lawyer who joined the Confederate Army and became a captain of the celebrated Valley Rangers of the Stonewall Brigade, only to become injured and ill with camp fever and return home to die in 1863 at age 23." The undertaker hired a crew of laborers to exhume the bodies. They found Captain Dovel buried in a cast-iron, bullet-shaped coffin with a glass window over his face. The hinged coffin was held shut by two large bolts.

Yount continues: "Aunt Bettie Post and my father were present when the iron casket was raised. The men dusted off the window, and there was Captain Dovel, looking as if he were merely asleep. He was buried in his Confederate uniform, with a crimson sash for decoration. Aunt Bettie asked the undertaker if he would open the casket for a moment, to enable her to see her uncle 'in full regalia.'

"The men unscrewed the screws and lifted the top." As soon as the air hit inside, there was a "mild, soundless implosion." The body disintegrated instantly into dust before their eyes.

Yount adds that Aunt Bettie rushed back to the house, and the laborers dropped their tools and ran off in all directions.

******

The Man Who Was Late for His Own Funeral

(Author's note: I am indebted to my fellow ghost writer, Ed Okonowicz of Elkton, Maryland, for the following true experience

– one of the zaniest, most bizarre tales, with unexpected twists, that I have heard. Ed writes mostly of the history and haunts of the Delmarva Coast. This one he collected in an interview a few years ago with a postmistress in a small town on the Eastern Shore. For privacy reasons, the town's exact location and the woman's full name, and the full names of others involved, are not disclosed. Her first name is Polly. Ed said she approached him after he gave a talk at a local library.)

Polly said she was at work at her small post office one afternoon when a woman she didn't know came up to the counter and asked for a package she had been expecting. Polly stepped into the back of the building to look for it. After searching for a few minutes the bell on her front counter began ringing loudly. She went back to the counter, and the woman, obviously agitated, demanded that her package be brought to her immediately.

Polly told her she couldn't find the package. This sent the woman into a rage. She said the package contained the ash remains of an "Uncle Wilbur" who had died in Michigan. His funeral service was to be held at the local cemetery within the hour. She said his grave had been dug and friends and relatives were already at the funeral parlor. What was she to do?

Polly decided to call around to neighboring town post offices to see if the package had been delivered to one of them by mistake. But before she could pick up the telephone, the woman told her to get a large official postal box. The woman then stormed out the front door and picked up a big stone from the front walkway. She brought it back to the counter, told Polly to seal it in the box, load it up with stamps, and to cancel the stamps with her date stamper.

Polly was stunned. The woman told her she would take the box directly to the cemetery and have it buried as is. Polly asked her if the mourners wouldn't want to open the box and bury what they thought was the urn inside. The woman said she would insist they bury the whole unopened box – that she couldn't bear to look inside it. Then she paid for the postage, told Polly she would be back in a few days to claim the real ash remains of Uncle Wilbur, and, in a huff, rushed out of the post office.

Less than a week later, the "Uncle Wilbur" package arrived. Polly placed it on a storage shelf in the back of the building, but neither the woman, or anyone else, came to claim him. There, "he" stayed for about a month. Then one day, Justine, a part-time employee at the post office, told Polly she heard a tapping sound coming from the storage area. Justine said she only heard it when she was up front. Whenever she went in the back to check on the source, the tapping stopped. Justine was very superstitious, so Polly told her it was just some tree branches banging against the back of the building when the wind blew.

A couple of weeks later a customer walked in one day when Justine was working. The woman asked Justine why she was playing her radio so loud. Justine then told her it was to drown out the sounds of the tapping noises she heard in the storage room. The woman told Justine that she, too, had heard the tapping the last time she was in the post office.

Just then, both women heard a loud crash in the back room. They ran to the doorway. They saw a box in the middle of the floor. It was Uncle Wilbur's box! It was a full 15 feet away from the shelf upon which it had been resting, so there was no way it could have fallen off the shelf and got to that point. How did it get there? The customer didn't wait to find out. She dashed out of the building, leaving her stamps and change on the counter.

Justine called Polly at home, and she came in. They opened the package and, inside, found an urn, apparently containing the remains of Uncle Wilbur. Justine, terribly frightened, said she was going to bring in some blessed candles and incense, and wear a special charm to ward off evil spirits.

After Justine left, Polly resealed the box and carried it to an outside shed where unclaimed parcels were stored. But this didn't stop the tapping. In fact, it not only increased in intensity, but grew progressively louder! It began to unnerve Polly. She thought about telling her regional manager, but decided not to, feeling he would think she was crazy. Finally, she told a close friend of hers, a local man named Henry. Henry had studied all kinds of psychic phenomena.

Henry felt that Uncle Wilbur must be disturbed that he had not been properly buried. He needed to be put to rest. So one dark night he and Polly took the urn up to the town cemetery and sprinkled his ashes over his grave site. They never heard the tapping sounds again.

But the saga doesn't end there. Polly says that no one ever came to claim Uncle Wilbur's package. However, a few weeks later Henry came into the post office and showed her a copy of an obituary of the deceased that had been printed in Michigan – the site from which the package had been shipped.

Turns out Uncle Wilbur had been a Baptist minister in Michigan, although he was a native of the Eastern Shore. That was why his remains had been sent back for interment. Then Henry and Polly speculated on the cause of the dead man's anxiety at having been left for so long in the post office. They at first had thought he was tapping because he wanted to be rightfully buried. But maybe there was another reason.

The post office building – 100 years ago – had been a seaside saloon and house of ill repute, frequented by hard-drinking sailors and watermen. Was the preacher upset at being held "prisoner" in such a place of evil? Or, after a lifetime of starchy strict upright living, did he want to be released in the building so he could have a good time with the wild spirits of the past?

One wonders.

(For a list of Ed Okonwicz's ghost books, write him at 1386 Fair Hill Lane, Elkton, MD 21921.)

A POTPOURRI OF PERCEIVED PHANTOMS

erception can be defined as a "mental image." Another definition is "quick, acute, and intuitive cognition."

Perception, however, can be very deceiving at times. There are, for instance, many, many cases where people have truly believed they have seen, or otherwise encountered a ghostly presence, when, in reality, there was a perfectly plausible and down-to-earth explanation for what they experienced.

Imaginations can run wild at times. Fear can panic thoughts. Moonlight and shadows can play tricks on aroused minds. Owls' screeches and howling dogs can axacerbate already jangled nerves, and cause a normally rational person to think irrationally. Who among us has not walked alone down a dark alley or a forest path at night, and upon hearing a sudden sound, or glimpsed sudden movement – not had the hair on the backs of our necks stand up?

Here, then, is a collection of ghosts that weren't ghosts, but were scary nevertheless.

We start with some incidents caused by humans.

The 'Corpse' that Talked Back

In his 1929 book, "The Mountains Redeemed," a sort of personal history of the hills and valleys of southwest Virginia, author Samuel Hurst tells of a young doctor who, a century or so ago, in his zeal to learn more about human anatomy, robs a grave to have a corpse to practice on, and is frightened out of his wits.

The poor fellow died and was buried out in some lonely country spot. The young 'doc' knew of his death and the place of burial. One night he hired someone's horse and buggy and went out alone and resurrected the 'stiff.' He sat him upright in the buggy, tying him to the back of the seat so he would maintain his rectitude and dignity.

"The 'couple' drove along without a word until they came to a way-side saloon, when doc feels that he needs some 'medicine' to calm his nerves. He gets out and goes into the saloon and gets a 'dram,' and takes a pint along with him for good measure and emergency.

"While he is in the saloon, someone who is 'on to' the doctor's game, quickly cuts the straps, lays the corpse privately aside, and gets up in the seat himself, and sits there with all the dignity of his predecessor. The doctor comes out, gets in, and taking the reins, quickly drives off.

"After going a short distance, he takes another drink, and, in the spirit of braggadocio, sticks the bottle up under the stiff's nose and says, 'Have a snort, old pard!'

"The stiff replies, 'I don't care a damn if I do!', whereupon the doctor immediately drops the driving reins, leaps unceremoniously from the buggy, and almost without awaiting to alight, picks up his feet and runs down the road as fast as a ghost-pursued man can make his pendulums vibrate!

"The 'ghost' drives on and never comes in sight of the fast-fleeing doctor. The doctor had to look elsewhere for bones. We are not sure but that he quit medicine and went into the ministry!"

******

The 'Unhaunted' Barn

In his 1975 book, "Say. . . . . Have I Told You?" Frank B. Rowlett, Jr., one of southwest Virginia's premier story tellers, describes a colorful incident that happened at an undisclosed location many years ago. It involved an old barn on an abandoned farm. The site was a favorite among local hunters after small game, and for young boys who liked to "go exploring" in the barn. Over time, however, the decrepit building acquired a reputation for being haunted.

Then one evening at the area's general store, a hunter told of his chilling experience at the barn. He had been out hunting rabbits, he said, and was heading home as darkness was falling. He stopped by the old barn to light his pipe. As he did, he heard "a terrible screaming." He opened the door to see what the cause was and said, "things began running around in there.," and "something white flitted by inside."

That was enough for him. He took off running and didn't stop until he got to the store. This man's word was taken seriously, because he was known throughout the county for his soberness and veracity.

Then, the next morning, two boys verified the account. They, too, said they had encountered a ghost. The day before they had been in the loft of the barn when, they said, "furry things started flying around them, and tried to grab them." They flung off the "creatures," scrambled down the ladder, and raced to the front door. But as they neared it, they said the door started opening by itself. They screamed out and then took off for the back door, and as they did, they heard "an awful howling."

These two simultaneous versions seemed to solidify the barn's haunting reputation, at least for awhile. But something struck the owner of the store as peculiar. He talked to the hunter and to the two boys, and then he went out to investigate the barn. After much thought on the matter, he came up with a perfectly rational explanation.

He figured the hunter came by the barn with his rabbits, while the boys were in the loft. He tossed the rabbits into the loft when he stopped to light his pipe, using both hands. The rabbits whizzed by the boys in the darkened loft, and they screamed. When the hunter then opened the door he caught a fleeting glimpse of the boys trying to escape, and thought they were ghosts. The howling the boys heard came from the hunter as he turned and ran toward the store.

******

The 'Specter' at the Seven Graves

Martin D. Julian told the following to WPA writer James Taylor Adams at East Stone Gap, October 27, 1941:

"When I was a boy, we lived near a place where seven soldiers (from the Civil War) were buried. The graves were on a knoll and the road passed right by them and then crossed a shallow creek. The Baptist church was up just above the graves and the Methodist church just below. One night they were holding a meeting up at the Baptist church and two of our neighbor boys, Arthur Gray and Robert Carmichial, had went. They admitted afterwards that they were drinking a little.

"They left the meeting and walked down the road. Came to

the seven graves, as the place was called, and one of them bantered to the other to climb upon a bank under some trees just across the creek from the graves and watch for the haint that was said to be seen there. They agreed, and clumb up on the bank and laid down. From where they were, they could see directly across the creek to the graves and the road coming over the rise by the cemetery.

"Meeting broke up and everybody went home. It must have been about midnight when the boys thought they heard something come over near the graves and looked, and there came a woman, or something, as they said, just like she was raising right up out of the graves. She, or whatever it was, was dressed in white from head to foot, and seemed to be just floating along.

"They watched it and it come right on the edge of the creek and was heading straight for where they were. One of them jumped up and started to run up the road, and the other right behind him. Just as they got started running, they heard a woman scream behind them, and they run that much the faster. It was a good two miles to where they lived, but they didn't stop till they got there. They were so exhausted that they both took down with fever and came very near dying.

"The strange part of it was that my sister, Hattie Julian, who was about 21 at the time, had a habit of walking in her sleep, and that night she had got out of bed, dreaming, she said, that she was going to meeting at the Baptist church, and walked up the road with nothing on but her night clothes. When she stepped into the water at the creek, it waked her, and she let out a scream.

"And that was the 'ghost' the boys got so scared at!"

******

A Voice from the Vault

In her delightful 1927 book, "Memoirs of a Poor Relation," Marietta Minnigerode Andrews writes about Virginia in the years after the Civil War. She was related to many of the more famous names in the commonwealth, and spins scores of anecdotes about a number of historic homes. One of these incidents, scary at first but later considered funny, took place at Oatlands, the plantation mansion in Loudoun County near Leesburg.

On one visit there as a child, Mrs. Andrews writes: "The family vault (containing the remains of Carter family members who once owned the house and grounds) is far down in the bottom of the terraced garden, deep among the cedars and hemlocks, draped with weeping willows – a dark and lonely spot. We children had a naughty way of pounding on the heavy, rusty iron door, beating a tattoo with our fists and calling to the ancestral dead: 'Come out, Misters Carters! Come out'!"

One evening, however, when she ventured into the garden to the vault, alone, she was terrified when the "deep sounds of a man's voice chilled the very blood in my veins – had he – could it be?"

Turned out to be Martin, the family gardener.

Mrs. Andrews apparently never talked about the encounter after that. She wrote: "I felt that this mysterious rendezvous at the vault should remain forever sealed and sacred."

******

When Seeing Isn't Believing

Author Grace Dunlop Ecker tells an entertaining anecdote in her 1951 book, "A Portrait of Old Georgetown." She called it a "delicious story." It occurred sometime in the early 1900s and concerned an "Aunt Peggy." Seems she was awakened one night about four a.m. when a cow somehow wandered through her gate and got into the yard. Aunt Peggy roused all five of her daughters and told them to go out and chase the cow away.

The girls, all dressed in flowing white night gowns, ran around in the yard trying to shoo the animal out the gate. Just then a milkman happened to be passing by, and when he saw the flitting gowns billowing in the breeze, he dropped his bottles and left the scene post-haste, believing he had seen a yard full of ghosts.

******

The next three items are strikingly similar, both in the events and the results. They all involve strange 'stirrings' at cemeteries.

Rising Up From the Tombstones

The following is excerpted from the October 1921 issue of "The Confederate Veteran," a magazine for southern survivors of the Civil War. It was related by a man named Jim Warden, who had served as a scout during the war.

"I had been on scout duty, and my command was operating in the vicinity where the town of Stafford is now located. My father's home was about 10 miles west of Stafford, and I took occasion to

visit the family one night and get a good square meal, though it was risky business. I hitched my horse back of the house in a thicket, and when the family retired for the night, mother gave me a large white cotton blanket, as the nights were kind of frosty, you know, and I came down to this old graveyard as a safe place to sleep.

"Well, I found a nice grassy bed right between two graves, whose large flat marble slabs had toppled over, and I lay down and had just gone into a dreamy snooze when I heard the clatter of a horse's hooves, and, looking toward the entrance, where once there had been an old gate, what was my terror when I distinguished the outline of a horseman riding directly toward where I lay. Great Scott! I pulled my revolver and quietly watched the intruder on my dreams. Then, as he approached to about 20 feet, he bent over and seemed to be looking at me, and there he sat on his horse, bending this way and that. I was confident he was trying to find my hiding place, for it was very dark.

"Then an idea seized me, and, wrapping the ample white blanket about me, I sat up. The horse gave a snort. I raised up with the white blanket fluttering about me and stepped up on one of the mounds. The stranger saw it. He gave one wild, despairing yell, and out of the cemetery he rushed in a mad gallop, and I lay down, convulsed.

"But listen: there is more. About 10 years ago I was riding past the same old graveyard, in company with a man who was raised not a thousand miles from this spot, when the companion said,

'Warden, do you believe in ghosts?'

"'No,' said I. 'Do you?'

"'You bet I do, Warden, and so would you if you had been with me once during the times of the war.'

"'Why,' said I, 'what about it?'

"He stopped right along about here, filled his pipe, and said in a deep, solemn voice: 'Warden, I always feel skeery when I come by this old graveyard, and I feel like something was crawling up my spine, and I kind of hate to tell it, but you and I were old scouts in 1861 and 1862. Well, sir, listen: One night I was out on scout duty near here and I lost my spur, and the lazy old nag I was mounted on was so slow that when I came to the gate yonder I rode in to get me a good sprout that I knew was growing out of the old neglected stumps.

"'Well, Warden, I was trying to break one off at the root and didn't want to dismount, when suddenly my old horse gave an unearthly snort, and as I turned to look, Holy Moses!, there arose out of one of those long graves a ghost ten feet high, flapping his wings and starting for me! Great Heavens, Warden! I'm scared when I think of it, and the sight of that ghost has haunted me all these years ever since.'

"And then I laughed and laughed until my sides fairly ached, and then I laughed some more. It was just too funny, and you are the very man I wanted to hear it. I told my companion all about it and detailed every incident until he was thoroughly convinced, and then he laughed. But the evil spell that had haunted him for all these long years had been broken."

******

'Ye Judgment Day Is Come!'

This incident occurred some distance north of Stafford and many years earlier. It was recorded in Alice Morse Earle's 1901 book, "Stage-Coach and Tavern Days," and involves an eccentric and most colorful Indian woman known as Sarah Boston. According to author Earle, Sarah "showed in her giant stature, her powerful frame, her vast muscular power, no evidence of a debilitated race or of enfeebled vitality. It is said she weighed over 300 pounds. Sarah dressed in short skirts, a man's boots and hat, and, like a true Indian, always wore a blanket over her shoulders in winter.

"Her great strength and endurance made her the most desired

farm-hand in the township to be employed in haying time, in wall-building, or in any heavy farm work. Her fill of cider was often her only pay for some powerful feat of strength, such as stone-lifting or stump-pulling. . . She begged cider at the tavern, and drank cider everywhere. 'The more I drink, the drier I am,' was a favorite expression of hers.

"Her insolence and power of abuse made her dreaded for domestic service." In short, Sarah was a much feared woman. And she often visited the local cemetery to pay her respects to near kin. It was at this site that Earle tells the following:

"A party of rollicking Yankee blades, bold with tavern liquor, pounded one night on the wooden gate of the old Grafton burying-ground, and called out in profane and drunken jest, 'Arise, ye dead, the judgment day is come!'

"Suddenly from one of the old graves loomed up in the dark the gigantic form of Sarah Boston, answering in a loud voice, 'Yes, Lord, I am coming!'

"Nearly paralyzed with fright, the drunken fellows fled, stumbling with dismay before this terrifying and unrecognized apparition."

******

Conversation with a Dead Man

In his 1927 book, "Tidewater Tales," author William Garrett tells of a character named "Charlie," who was a slick salesman in his day. The episode took place one night early in the 20th century at a country store in King and Queen County.

After making his sale at the store, Charlie waited around for someone to give him a ride. He apparently had no means of conveyance of his own. It was very dark and raining hard. After awhile an old Negro known as "Zack," stopped in the store. Zack was talked into taking Charlie in his buggy, but Zack was only going part way. So Charlie quickly concocted a plan that would take him all the way to his destination.

As they rode off, Charlie asked Zack if he believed in ghosts. Zack answered: "I hardly know what I believe on that subject. I've seen strange sights in my life, but then I don't say that any of these was ghosts." He then was asked if he was afraid of ghosts, and he replied, "I can't say that I is exactly that, but, still, I ain't looking for them night or day.."

Charlie said the reason he was asking was because he had lost a very dear friend recently, and he would like to stop by the graveyard where he was buried – which was on their way – because he wanted "to have a talk" with his departed friend.

"Is he dead?" Zack asked, his eyes wide open.

"Oh, yes, and he has been buried several weeks."

"W-W-Well, Zack stammered, "how you going to talk to him if he is dead and buried?"

Charlie told Zack that was why he had asked him if he was afraid of ghosts. "You see," he said, "I have a great power over these poor wanderers of the dark and stormy night, and it helps me to call them up and soothe them with a friendly talk."

Zack looked at Charlie as if he were an escaped lunatic. Just then, they came upon a church, and Charlie drove the buggy right up to the cemetery gate next to it. Zack sat as quiet as a statue, freezing with fright. Charlie told him he saw his friend. "Be perfectly quiet," he told Zack. "Your horse is safe and so are you if you keep perfectly quiet. One sound and all is lost."

He then called out to a grave site in the pitch blackness: "Harvey, Harvey, come up Harvey! That is right. Come right along Harvey. . . A little higher, just a little higher. There you are. Come to me, Harvey!"

As Garnett wrote: "There was a rush and a rattle and a bang and a tearing of old clothes, and the quickest disappearance from that buggy ever seen before. Zack went as hard as his old feet could carry him through the woods in a straight line for his home. Charlie stood and watched and laughed until he was sore. He got in that buggy and went on to Courtney's Store in short order. He then sent the horse and buggy back to the old man and fully remunerated him for the use of the horse and buggy.

"But Zack said, 'nothing in this world would pay him for that ghost coming out of that grave that night and for all the skin he scratched off himself running through the woods'."

******

The Non-Ghost of Dead Man's Hollow

Sometimes a person can be his or her own worse enemy when it comes to ghostly perception. Consider this poor fellow, whose plight was described by Dr. George E. Wiley in his 1906 book, "Plantation Tales." This particular episode involved a well-known doctor in the area sometime in the latter half of the 19th century. On a stormy night, the doctor had been called out to a remote cabin in the woods to attend a man's severely burned leg.

"He dressed the burn without comment, and hastily left the house and started back home. Looking to the west, he saw dark clouds gathering; there was going to be a storm. He knew it would not do to wait any longer, as the mountain streams rose very rapidly during a heavy storm. Leading his horse to the bank, he mounted, fixed himself well in the saddle, and put spurs to him. The horse hesitated, drew back, wheeled about, reared and refused to go in; but by whip and spur, he finally made the plunge and went in up to the saddle.

"The doctor was alarmed; but there was nothing to do but trust to luck and push ahead, when, to his great relief, he found the water getting shallow, and in a few moments he struck the bank. Though the storm was rapidly approaching, he was cold and wet to the skin, and his saddle pockets with the medicine gone to physic the fishes, he did not care.

"He soon found the road that led from the river through a long, dark gorge called 'Dead Man's Hollow.' It was said that a man had been murdered in this gulch many years ago, and the place was haunted; but the doctor felt so much relieved at his escape from the river that he thought nothing of the dark, gloomy gulch and gruesome stories he had heard. He thought it must be true that the 'darkest hours are just before dawn,' for the darkness was intense; the clouds had thickened, the thunder had grown more distinct, the storm would soon be on.

"He urged his horse along as fast as he could with safety, when he began to hear the leaves rustle and the twigs crack, as if some animal was walking in the leaves near him. He peered into the darkness, but saw nothing, but keeping his eyes turned in the direction of the sound, he presently saw what appeared to be two balls of fire, evidently the eyes of some wild animal, following him. He shouted at the top of his voice, hoping to frighten it away; but the blazing eyes only seemed to stand still.

"He urged his horse, which now appeared to be thoroughly frightened, when suddenly he stopped, and he could feel him quivering in every muscle. Urge as he would with whip and spur, the horse would not budge. The air seemed to have a strange chill about it, and he heard the animal, whatever it was, bound away through the brush.

"He put his hand down on his horse's shoulder; he was trembling like a leaf and wet with sweat. There seemed to be something awful about to happen. Glancing over his shoulder, he either saw, or thought he saw, a long, bony hand on each of his shoulders; and, looking over his shoulder, a face covered with long, white beard and head with snow-white hair, and in the sunken caverns of his face – glowed two fiery eyeballs, like those he had seen on the mountainside!

"He tried to scream, his voice had left him. He tried to spring from his trembling horse; he was as one paralyzed.

"Suddenly, there came a flash of lightning and a crash of thunder which shook the mountains to their very foundation; the horse sprang forward with a sudden bound, which came near throwing the doctor to the ground.

"By the flash of lightning he saw a white cow in the road, which evidently had frightened the horse and made him stop.

"The nearest house the other side of Dead Man's Hollow was Captain Smyth's. Day was just beginning to dawn when the doctor rode up to the captain's gate and knocked at the door . . .
The captain said, 'you are as pale as a ghost; are you sick?'

"The doctor was quick-witted. He saw at a glance (in a mirror) what his ghost had been. He had laid his hat down in some flour which Arnett (the man he had tended) had been using on his burnt leg, and had gotten it on his coat and shoulders.

"The blazing eyes of the catamount or wild cat he had just seen were photographed on the retina, and in the state of his excited nerves, easily transferred to the face of the ghost of Dead Man's Hollow, whose snowy beard and hair was his white hat brim, and his bony hands (were) his flour-sprinkled shoulders!

"Captain Smyth, (the doctor said) you usually keep a little apple brandy. Can you give me a toddy?"

******

Sometimes the power of suggestion is so strong that even harmless objects can lead one to believe they have experienced something out of the supernatural. Here then is a quartet of such occasions.

The Moon Flower Phantom

In 1908 the Wilson family – mother, father, son Matt, 10, and daughters Ollie, nine, and Elvie, eight, lived on a farm near the Redbird River in southwestern Virginia. As usual in those days, the children were each assigned specific chores. Ollie and Elvie didn't particularly care for one of theirs. It was to go out in the dying sunlight of the day and fetch "Ole Moll," the family cow. The girls didn't like this because Moll was a contrary animal, and they often had a difficult time getting her to leave the lush green pastures and head for the barn. And if they were late for supper, they inevitably got a good scolding.

In addition, they had to pass by an old abandoned cabin on their way; a cabin locals said was haunted. Their brother, Matt, told them it was the specter of a killer who murdered an unsuspecting Indian with a hatchet. Matt, who took perverse pleasure in scaring his sisters, told them the man had been so mean the devil wouldn't take him, so his ghost roamed about around the old cabin, still looking for unwary victims.

One evening, as the sun was dropping behind the mountains, Ollie and Elvie were having an especially difficult time getting Old Moll to move. They prodded her with tobacco sticks, and, as dusk settled, they came over a rise and saw, in the distance, the haunted cabin. Little Elvie froze in her tracks. Her mouth opened wide and her eyes seemed big as saucers. When Ollie turned to see was Elvie was staring at, she, too, turned to stone.

There, by the front porch of the cabin, was a pale apparition – a luminous white figure as tall as a man!

Ollie grabbed Elvie's hand in a frantic effort to make a run for it. But Elvie was transfixed. She wouldn't, or couldn't budge. Finally, tugging desperately, Ollie managed to slowly drag her terrified sister along. Old Moll was just ahead of them, and a few feet beyond the cow was the eerie figure.

Ollie started to recite the Lord's prayer, but she couldn't remember all the words. When they were closest to the cabin, both girls stopped, closed their eyes, and hugged each other tightly. Remembering the stories Matt had told them, they trembled in fear, expecting a bloody hatchet to come raining down on them at any instant.

After a minute or two, when nothing happened, Ollie opened her eyes and peeked over toward the cabin. Then she smiled and told Elvie to open her eyes. "Look," she said, "Old Moll is eating the ghost!"

The girls then broke out in nervous laughter. The apparition they thought they had seen was just a row of moon flowers – thick white blossoms that were climbing up the trellis beside the porch. Someone must have planted these night bloomers after the rose bushes were frozen. In the hazy, darkening distance they had appeared to the girls as a whitish entity that, combined with their runaway imaginations, had created a most frightening vision.

A little later, safely seated at the dinner table, Ollie and Elvie told no one of their encounter at the cabin. It was their secret.

******

The Stirrups that Stirred Things Up

At Tudor Hall in Dinwiddie, outside of Petersburg, Mrs. Thomas Diehl liked to tell a colorful story about the ghosts in her home that never were. The house predates the Civil War and its owners fled when some fierce skirmishes were waged in the area. For a time, Tudor Hall served as a hospital for Union soldiers, and, according to a legend that has been passed down for generations, some of them still return to march at night across the attic floor.

At least that's what Mrs. Diehl's father used to say, although she admits he was a great tease. One night before she was born, two young women relatives were visiting and spent the night in a room close to the stairway that led to the attic. The stairway is of "perfectly beautiful pine and long and winding."

Mrs. Diehl's father had tantalized the women after dinner with the story of the military ghosts, and, coincidentally, that night as they lay in bed they heard a noise that "sounded exactly like a lot of people marching across the attic." They were understandably frightened and called the man of the house, who by this time was scared himself.

Together, they finally managed enough courage to investigate. They discovered a saddle that had been placed on the railing above the stairs. It had fallen and the wooden stirrups hit each step on the way down, sounding like marching men descending the stairs.

Mrs. Diehl says her father was reluctant to talk about the ghosts after that.

******

The Meal Sack Spirit

In her master's thesis on Carroll County folklore, written in 1955, Ninevah Jackson Willis recorded the following anecdote, based on an interview with a young woman.

"Speaking of the Cloud Road, we used to hear so many ghost tales about that place. Once, two girls and I decided to scare a friend, so just as we got to the gate of the Cloud graveyard, I said, in an eerie voice, 'Looky, there's old Jim Cloud!'

"Just then we heard a noise behind us. We looked around and Mark Bowman was coming home from the mill with a meal sack on his shoulder. All we could see was the white sack dancing along in the moonlight. I didn't run, but I passed three other girls who were running, and we didn't stop until we got home and hid our heads under Ma's apron!"

******

A Tangle with a 'Spook Tree'

The following is excerpted from a letter sent to the author by Calvin Webb of Lauren Fork, Virginia:

"One evening some years ago I stopped by to visit with my aunt, who was in her 70s then. She told me old tales about witches and the sort. I laughed at her foolishness, and she became stern with me. She said that if I believed in the Bible I would know there is a Devil and that he has helpers, too.

"That night as I was heading home, it was really dark. Not a star or moon in the sky when I left her house. I was really tense and wound up. I was thinking about the tales I had just heard, and the pitch black night didn't help."

(At this point, Calvin thought he had an encounter with something from another world. He said it felt like someone's giant arms

had grabbed him, and something was banging him on the back of his head.)

"I kicked, bit and spit with all my might. I fought tooth and nail for what seemed like several minutes."

(Calvin thought he was literally fighting for his life. In reality, he had walked into a tree with low hanging branches, and had gotten all tangled up in the darkness. He was thrashing about with limbs and branches.)

"Finally," he concludes, "I realized what had happened. The next day I went back. There were needles and limbs everywhere. I tried to tromp back the roots, but everyone wondered what had happened to that old tree for years. I never told."

******

Smashing through the Screen Door

It is seldom mentioned or referred to today, but years ago the natural phenomenon known as "jack-o-lantern" was at times misinterpreted and thought by some to be a "ghost light." Jack-o-lantern, or ignis fatuus, is a light that occasionally appears in the night over marshy ground, and often is attributable to the combustion of gas from decomposed organic matter. It was commonplace back in the days when most Virginians lived in rural areas. Sightings of such "marsh gas" could sometimes prove to be quite scary, especially to a person out alone at night.

Such apparently was the case 70-odd years ago near Ebony, halfway between Marion and Abingdon, in Brunswick County. "When my grandparents lived at the Elam House there in 1930, the jack-o-lanterns used to bounce all around the wood pile," writes Maxine Connor, who now lives in Garysburg, North Carolina. Maxine says these took the form of round balls of light. "When my grandfather would stay out late drinking, the jack-o-lanterns would beat and bang on the windows sometimes at night. My grandmother used to put her four kids in bed around her when this happened.

"Once my grandmother's brother was walking down the path to the house. He had his banjo with him, picking on it. Gran heard him coming and she went out on the porch to meet him. One of the round balls of light bounced onto the neck of the banjo. He threw the instrument down and took off running toward the house, calling for someone to open the screen door. Gran couldn't understand what he was saying.

"He ended up running past her and went straight through the closed screen door into the house, and didn't stop running until he was in the kitchen!"

******

There have even been times when the fear of a perceived ghost has caused physical harm to the person involved – in the following instances, self-inflicted harm.

Hand and Foot

Nearly a century ago a man named Hand moved into a house that was suspected of being haunted, near the tiny community of Tyaskin on the Eastern Shore. Hand knew a little of the history, including the fact that no family would stay in the house long before moving out, often on very short notice. But the price was right, and Hand believed he could cope with whatever situation arose.

He didn't have long to wait to test his mettle. Within a few weeks, strange noises issued from the attic. As the nights passed, the sounds seemed to get closer, coming down the attic stairs. Finally, Hand grabbed a lantern one evening and decided to find out the cause of the unexplained disturbances.

He met a huge rat on the stairs. Startled, he instinctively kicked hard at the rodent, which quickly disappeared. Hand, however, broke his foot in the process, and he moved his family out of the house a week later.

******

Never Shoot a Ghost!

The following account is said to have actually occurred a few years after the end of the Civil War, although it is impossible to verify the date or the facts. It is one of those time-honored legends that have been passed down, family to family, through the years. And while, in a sense, it is not funny, it is nevertheless a choice bit of backwoods humor.

It involved a man called "Grandpappy Sparks." He was known throughout the region, in southwest Virginia, as a coon hunter. There was nothing he loved better. One night around midnight he woke up from a sound sleep feeling "kinda quare." A beam of moonlight shone down through a hole in the roof, and illuminated the room.

Grandpappy looked down, and then rubbed his eyes in disbelief. At the foot of his bed he saw "something white and quare fluttering back and forth." He always kept his trusty rifle by his side, even when he slept. He grabbed it, aimed it toward the foot of the bed, and yelled out, "Speak if you're human!" There was only silence. Grandpappy repeated the warning, "Speak if you're human!" When again there was no reply, he aimed the shotgun and blasted away.

He blew off all five of the toes on his right foot!

******

Never Shoot a Ghost! (II)

John Lipps of Wise, Virginia, told the following to Works Progress Administration writer James Taylor Adams, on August 28, 1941.

"About 40 years ago I was working at a sawmill near Damascus. I lived in town and just out at the edge of Damascus is the old Mock graveyard. I had to pass right by it every night and morning and I had to go before day and come back home after dark. Everybody said the graveyard was haunted. All sorts of haints had been seen there, they said. I hadn't ever seen anything, and I didn't believe there was anything to see.

"But one night I was coming in a little later than usual, and just as I got right against the graveyard, out stepped something white and stopped right in the middle of the road. I had always heard it said that you couldn't touch or shoot a ghost. All right, I said, if you are a haint I'll see if I can hit you. So I just out with my pistol and 'bang!'

"At the crack of the gun it jumped about ten feet in the air and come down with a thud, and I seen it kicking and struggling like something a dying. I'll confess I was a little shaky, but I picked up my nerve and marched up to it.

"What do you reckon it was? Not a thing in the world but a big sheep! I didn't do a thing but find out who it belonged to and paid the man for it. And since then I have never shot at a ghost!"

******

Only an Angel

One hundred and fifty years ago, historic Christ Church, near Irvington, was in sad repair. Organized religion at the time was in disfavor and the church was deserted, a mere shell of its former prominence. The only "tenants" during this period were occasional

horseback riders, who, when caught out in the vicinity when a storm broke, sought shelter under the church's roof.

According to author Louise Dawe, who wrote a little booklet, "To Irvington with Love," there was a family named Angel living nearby. One night, during a particularly heavy downpour, a lone rider clopped his horse through the open church door to dry off. Before he could dismount, he heard a voice coming from the darkened gallery. Startled, he called out, "Who's there?"

Whereupon the voice responded, "Only one of us Angels."

The rider spurred his horse and departed at top speed.

******

The Dancing Ghost Exposed

Brantley Henderson, author of "Only the Happy Memories -- Reminiscences of a Virginia Boyhood" -- published a half century ago -- tells a marvelous tale on himself that is both amusing and insightful of just how prevalent enduring superstitions and folk beliefs were in rural parts of the commonwealth long ago. This particular incident which Henderson describes occurred in the South Boston area about a hundred years ago when he was a young boy. His father then ran a country store and on this occasion young Henderson was accompanied by his older brother, Bubba. They were asked by their father to walk down a dark road at night to deliver a message to a man in a cabin. Here's what Henderson wrote:

"Wandering around at night was no fun to two hant-minded shavers, but Pa's word was always a command. Bubba's popping eyes looked at me, and I looked at him. We didn't speak. Slowly and nervously we pulled on our breeches . . . and headed down the road . . . There were three small houses down the side road from our home. Colored families lived in the first two, but Mr. Charles Jennings, a big, fat white man, lived in the third, and that's the one to which we were headed.

"Uncle Lige Marshall lived in the middle one for many years, but two weeks before, Lige's grown daughter, Emma, died, and he promptly moved away. Colored people were then so afraid of hants or 'sperits,' they wouldn't live in a house in which a recent death had occurred. During the day Mr. Raleigh White had thoroughly scrubbed and cleaned this house.

"Once again the sky was clear and the moon was shining in full power. Bubba and I were walking down the road side by side.

The first house was occupied by Robert Thornton; living, breathing people were within its walls. We got by that one in good shape. But in the middle house, Emma had recently died and, except for the probability of her 'sperit' being around, it was empty. Strange indeed to say, I had not thought of Emma; I was extremely hant-conscious, and not for a million dollars would I have walked near that house alone, but Bubba was a big boy (then 13) and I felt safe by his side.

". . . We were within 100 feet of the house where Emma had died when Bubba suddenly stopped, raised his face to the sky and shouted, 'Oh, Lordy!' He remained as motionless as a statue for perhaps 20 seconds, then suddenly whirled and lit out for Pa's store at the speed of a deer. With every step he yelled, 'Oh, Lordy, oh, Lordy.'

"I had seen nothing scary and had heard no frightening sound, but from his actions I knew that Bubba had seen a whole flock of hants. I didn't take time to figure the situation out; the time had come to run as fast as I could to safety. What scared me was I couldn't keep up with Bubba. Whatever it might be that was about to get us, and it was sure to be hants, I was the one who would be got because I was 50 feet behind and losing ground at every step of Bubba's long legs. I should have been saving my breath to run faster, but I joined his call to the Lord for help.

"We must have been heard more than a mile away. Pa reached the door and threw it open just as Bubba cleared the steps and landed three feet within the room. Five seconds later I was safe inside, too. Bubba was wringing his hands, his eyes popped out of their sockets, and he was still yelling, 'Oh, Lordy.' Pa was saying, 'what on earth has happened?'

"Bubba kept saying, 'Oh, Lordy, oh Lordy, Pa, oh, Lordy, Pa..' I was shaking, my hair standing on end, and my eyes were bulging, but I wasn't saying a word. Getting no information from Bubba, Pa turned to me and said, "Brantley, can you tell me what happened?' 'I don't know, sir. Ask Bubba.' 'You were yelling, too.' 'Yes, sir, but I was just helping Bubba.'

"Neighbors who lived not more than a half mile from our home began arriving. Those who lived at greater distances appeared a few minutes later to find out what in tarnation had happened. Bubba was still crying and muttering, 'Oh, Lordy.' With a crowd of men standing around as protectors, the quivering of his lips and chin somewhat lessened. He stopped wringing his hands, and the color began returning to his face.

"For the hundredth time Pa asked, 'What in the world got after you?' (Bubba was finally able to speak.) 'With a white sheet over her head and body, Uncle Lige's Emma . . . was dancing in the middle of the floor!' Several of the white men laughed at Bubba's answer, but the eyes of the colored brethren widened as they knowingly looked at one another. (Two men) offered to go down to Lige's house to find out, if possible, what the young gentlemen had seen that looked like Emma's ghost dancing a jig.

"To the colored men present, what folly there was did not lie in Bubba's tale, but in the investigation by the two men. Everybody knew that hants lived in houses where people die, and to them it was perfectly natural that Emma's spirit should return to the room it had known so well.

"It wasn't long before the two men returned." What had happened? The men discovered
that earlier in the day Mr .White had left the doors and windows of the house open, hoping that air would dry the floors and walls during the night.

"A powder keg in which the family had grown flowers was sitting on a fence post directly in front of an open door facing east. Loosely wrapped in a newspaper, Mr .White had left the
remains of his lunch on the powder keg, and the ends of the paper were fluttering in the breeze. The full moon, then about an hour high, cast the shadows made by the flapping paper through the open door.

"A perfectly simple and understandable thing had caused a lot of trouble, and scared two red-headed boys out of five years' growth!"

******

The Scare that Broke a Nose

In his 1967 book, "God, Man, Salt Water and the Eastern Shore," William Tawes tells of a rather painful, yet amusing incident that once happened to his "Aunt Bertie" and "Uncle Jim." Living in a small, remote town on the shore, Bertie arose one night after they had gone to bed and shook her husband and told him that she heard a noise downstairs and thought someone was in the house. Jim got up, grabbed his pistol, and, trembling, cautiously crept down the front stairs.

Everything was "dark as pitch," so when he reached the hallway, he walked on toward the kitchen with his arms outstretched in front of him, as a sleepwalker might do. Unbeknownst to him, however, the kitchen door was ajar, and his arms extended on both sides of it without touching anything. Another step and he smashed his nose smack into the projecting edge of the door. The collision temporarily blinded him and momentarily paralyzed him with an excruciatingly sharp pain. He let out an unearthly yell.

It frightened Bertie and she came running down the back stairway, approaching the kitchen from the opposite direction. When the stars cleared under Jim's eyelids, he looked up, and in the dark all he could make out was a figure in a white nightgown. It was, of course, Bertie, but he couldn't distinguish her features. He screamed again, and, instinctively, flung his pistol at the figure.

Fortunately, Bertie ducked, and upon a review of the situation, they both thanked the Lord that Jim, for whatever reason, threw the pistol instead of firing it.

******

The Figure In White

Charles McFaddin, a Lexington historian, tells a funny story on himself. He says many years ago there was an eccentric and egotistical local minister named Vanderslice, who bought some land and built a church with his own money. Whenever the preacher, who always dressed in a white suit, wanted to make a point in his sermons, he would raise both hands high above his head.

And when Reverend Vanderslice died, since it was his own church, he decreed that he be buried under the alter. His wish was carried out, but it caused a perplexing problem. Congregation members swore that sometimes on moonlit nights they could see the apparition of the reverend standing behind the pulpit with his arms raised. This caused such a great deal of consternation that the brethren decided to built another church just down the street, leaving Vanderslice and his ghost abandoned.

After a period of decades, this "new" church fell into decay and eventually was bought and made into an automobile tire store. Charles says that when he was a child, his grandfather would drive him up the street by the store and tell him to look through the windows of the store as they passed by.

"We would hit a bump in the road and the car's headlights would flash through the windows, and I swear I saw a white apparition standing in the corner with its arms raised," Charles says. "I thought it was the Reverend Vanderslice, and I wondered how he got there, since he was buried in the old church up the street."

Years later, now a young man, Charles figured it out. What he was seeing was a model of the "Michelin Man," the famous white figure used by the tire company in its television commercials and newspaper advertisements!

'APPARITIONS' OF ANIMALS (AND OTHER CREATURES)

here are innumerable incidents of the paranormal involving animals, birds, and other creatures. It has been a long-standing belief, for instance, especially in the mountains and hollows, that a howling dog at night signifies the impending death of someone in the family. The same is true if a bird flies in an open window. There have been sightings of allegedly supernatural beasts, such as the Mothman, Big Foot, and others. Psychic pets have warned their masters of approaching disasters, and even saved lives. Other animals have been reported to have communicated with their owners after they had died.

And, there are scores of examples where animals, and other things, were thought to have been spirits from another world. Some of these cases are downright amusing.

The Furry Ghost in the Garret

The following is excerpted from the March 1851 issue of the "Southern Literary Messenger," which was edited and published in Richmond.

"A youth, about 14 years of age, was sent to pass some weeks of his summer holidays with a great aunt, who lived in one of the old counties of the Old Dominion. The venerable lady occupied one of those great mansion houses, memorials of the colonial aristocracy of Virginia, built of imported bricks, full of staircases and passages, and with rooms enough to accommodate half a dozen families, and scores of individual guests, when congregated for some high festival.

"But at this time it was almost deserted. The old lady and her grand-nephew were the only white persons within its walls. She occupied a bedroom on the first floor; our hero slept in the story next to the garret; and the servants were all in the basement. During the day, his time passed merrily enough. Horses, dogs and guns – boating and fishing – filled up the hours with sports. . .

"But the nights hung heavily. His aunt always went to bed at an early hour. The few books in her library were soon exhausted; and the short evenings of summer seemed to his sleepless eyes to be stretched out interminably. Now and then a gossip with some old Negroes, who had grown gray in the family, beguiled him with snatches of the history of the former occupants of the hall; and these narratives, as might be anticipated, were plentifully sprinkled with incidents of the superstitious character in which such old crones delight.

"One night, he had lain in bed a long time, courting in vain a relief from ennui in sleep. He had listened, till he was tired, to the ticking of the antique clock, to the whistling of the wind about the clusters of chimneys, and the echoes that repeated and prolonged every sound in the interior of the house, through its vast and empty spaces. The latter class of noises had entirely ceased; and the profound stillness that pervaded the mansion was broken only by the monotonous voice of the clock, which told him how slowly the weary minutes were passing by.

"He had thought over more than one tradition of the olden time, as it had been related to him, with its concomitants of a supernatural description; until, in spite of his better reason and his fixed disbelief in such things, he found himself growing nervous and uncomfortable. He began to fancy that he saw strange things in the uncertain moonlight, and was almost afraid to look at them steadily enough to undeceive himself.

"Suddenly, he heard, right over his head in the garret, a dull knocking sound, which traveled back and forth, now in this direction and now in that, with a succession of thumps. Anon he thought he could distinguish something like a stifled voice; and this impression was confirmed when the knocking got opposite the door of the garret, whence it came down the stairway and through the passage, unobstructed, to his room.

"A wild, unearthly cry, uttered as if by a person choked or muffled, and expressive of painful suffering, smote upon his ear. He started up in bed; and at this instant the sound began to descend the stairs. At first, it came down two or three steps with successive thumps – then it seemed to roll over and over, with a confused noise of struggling and scratching – and so on, with an alternation of these sounds until it reached the floor of the passage. Here the dull knocking was resumed as it had been first heard in the garret, rambling hither and thither, at one time approaching the chamber door, till the poor boy strained his eyes in instant expectation of witnessing the entry of some horrible shape.

"But it passed by and at last arrived at the head of the next flight of stairs, where it recommenced the descent after the manner already described. At intervals rose the same stifled wailing, so full of mortal terror and agony, that it almost froze the marrow in his bones.

"When he was assured by the sound that the traveler had arrived at the floor below him, he mustered courage, and by a great effort jumped out of bed, huddled on his clothes, and hurried to the head of the stairs, armed with an old sword that hung in his bedroom, and which had probably seen service in the Revolution or the old French and Indian War. But he had no mind to encounter his mysterious enemy at close quarters, and contented himself with following its progress at a safe distance, and peeping over the balusters in the hope of catching sight of it.

"In this, however, he succeeded only so far, as to get one glimpse, as it passed a window, of something with an enormous and shapeless head; and the slow chase was kept up, till he found himself at the head of the steps leading down to the basement, while his ghostly disturber was at the foot, thumping and scratching at the kitchen door, and uttering the same indescribable cries as at first.

"Two or three of the servants had been aroused by the din, and were crouched together in the furthest corner, trembling with fear, and in momentary expectation of suffering death, or something still more dreadful. At last the latch of the door gave way to the repeated assaults of the unwelcome visitor, and he rolled into the middle of the floor, in the full blaze of the fire light, and under the very eyes of the appalled domestics.

"The mystery was at an end – the ghost exposed – and an explosion of frantic mirth succeeded to the breathless terror which oppressed them.

"An old gray tom cat, as it turned out, in his rambles through the house, had chanced to find in the garret a large gourd, in which the housemaids kept grease for domestic uses. Into the opening of the gourd Tom had worked his head with some difficulty, and without duly considering how he was to get it out again. When he attempted to do this, he found himself tightly grasped by the ears and jaws, and secured in a cell which became every instant more intolerable.

"Hence his struggles to escape – hence his unearthly and smothered cries – and hence the extraordinary varieties of locomotion by which he accomplished his long journey from the top of the house to the bottom. Our hero drew from the issue of this adventure a confirmed resolution against a belief in the supernatural; and detailed the particulars next morning, with great unction, to his good old aunt, who had slept comfortably through the whole of the uproar!"

******

The Chair that Rocked by Itself

There persists a legend that a woman was murdered in the late 1800s at the Yellow House Inn in Port Republic, a few miles west of Weyer's Cave about midway between Harrisonburg and Waynesboro. It was said that her beheaded spirit would appear on the Inn's front porch and rock in a chair. It was further said that she especially liked to appear in this apparitional form on Halloween.

Sometime prior to 1914, because that is when the Yellow House Inn burned to the ground, three brave young men decided they were going to "face down" the ghost one Halloween. So when it became dark they sauntered up to the porch, sat down in rocking chairs, and waited. When nothing happened for several hours, they nodded off to sleep at about 1 a.m. Soon after, a neighborhood tom cat jumped into another rocking chair to join them.

Later, one of the men's loud snoring apparently spooked the cat and it leaped out of the chair, pushing off its hind legs. The men then awoke, saw the empty chair rocking back and forth, and ran from the Inn as fast as their legs would carry them!

******

'Killed' by a Rabbit!

Dr. R. A. Smith of White Stone, Virginia, told the following entertaining incident which occurred in July 1863 near the Bull Run Battlefield.

"We had not advanced more than a third of the distance when the order came to fall flat on the ground. Our colonel had learned that there were many thousands of Yankees between us and the battery. Young James Manning stood behind a tree instead of obeying the order. A solid cannon ball weighing 12 pounds cut the tree down and cut him in two. He was the first man of our company killed.

"Many of our men saw this shocking sight, and among them was a captain, a wonderfully good man and a Methodist preacher. During the commotion a rabbit had been frightened out of his hiding place and was running hither and thither, and at last jumped with all force against the captain's side.

"He whirled over and cried that a ball had killed him and asked his men to send his body home. They told him nothing had touched him but a rabbit. This did not convince him, and he did his level best to die anyway. Failing in this effort, he just disappeared, and we never saw him again."

******

A Descent into Hell

This item is excerpted from the March 1851 issue of the Southern Literary Messenger.

"A laborer, on his way homeward about nightfall, was passing along the outskirts of a little village, when his ear was assailed by repeated groans, which seemed to issue out of the very ground beneath his feet. Looking about him, and listening, he presently discovered that they proceeded from an old well, which had been abandoned, and was half filled with rubbish.

"Approaching the edge of it, he called aloud, but received no answer, except the same groans, which were uttered at intervals, with a hollow reverberation, that appeared to die away in subterranean passages. To see anything below was impossible; and the man set off at once to announce this strange occurrence, and seek assistance from the nearest houses.

"The alarm spread rapidly; and, in a little while, a busy crowd was collected at the spot, with torches, ropes, and other implements, for the purpose of solving the mystery, and releasing the unknown sufferer. A windlass (a machine for hoisting or hauling) and bucket were hastily procured, and rigged up; and one, more adventurous than his neighbors, volunteered to descend.

"They let him down about 20 feet, until he reached the bottom, which he declared to be completely covered by a large barrel, upon which he found firm footing. At this time, the noise had ceased and the newcomers were disposed to question the truth of what had been told them. But those who had first reached the place stoutly and angrily reasserted the reality of what they had heard. The first explorer had been drawn up almost to the top, when the groans were renewed, to the discomfiture of the skeptics, and the dismay of some of the bystanders.

"Dark hints were conveyed in smothered whispers from one to another. A few were observed to steal out of the circle, and silently move off towards their homes. None showed any particular inclination to repeat the descent in their own persons. But, at last, two or three, more resolute than the rest, determined, 'at all hazards and to the last extremity,' to know what was beneath the barrel.

"A pair of shears was sent for, such as are used for hoisting heavy packages into warehouses. Another descent was made, and, in spite of groans that might have shaken the nerves of Pilgrim himself, the shears were securely hitched on either side of the barrel. Several pairs of strong arms were applied to the windlass, but all their efforts proved fruitless for a time. It seemed as if the barrel had been anchored to the rock-fast foundations of the earth.

"At last, however, it yielded a little; and with a slow, interrupted motion, and a harsh, scraping sound, an empty barrel, with no heading, was detached from its fastenings, and then brought up rapidly to the top.

"Once more, a daring fellow went down, armed to the teeth, and giving repeated injunctions to his assistants to turn very slowly, and hold on hard. He encountered at the bottom a formidable animal indeed, at least in such a situation.

"It was no other than a cow, jammed into the lowest part of the well, with her branching horns pointing directly to the sky above. The poor beast, indulging a natural taste, had thrust her head into an empty salt barrel. Her horns had stuck fast in the sides, and retreating blindly, in her efforts to escape, she had backed down the dry well, dragging the barrel after her, which fitted so closely to the walls of the pit, as to break the force of her fall.

"With some difficulty, the poor creature was extricated from her sad plight, without injury!"

******

The Haunt in the Chinquepin Bushes

John Heatwole, the gifted author and folklorist of the Shenandoah Valley, tells of a most humorous incident which occurred in Waynesboro back in the years when it was a small village.

There had been a brutal murder. A woman named Mary Short had been found lying on her bed, with her throat cut and a razor by her side on the pillow. Her husband was strongly suspected, but his guilt was never proven.

Consequently, when a number of residents reported seeing the wraith of a woman lingering on the rough-hewn streets late at night, it was assumed that it was the ghostly figure of Mary Short, seeking justice for her cruel death.

So popular was this belief that very few people would even venture through that part of town after sundown. Joseph Morrison was one of these. It was said he feared no one. However, on one particularly dark night, as he wandered home, "a pale, ghostly and disembodied face rose up among the chinquepin bushes right beside him." Morrison ran home at lightning speed and breathlessly told what he had seen.

A short time later, a few of his friends went out to see things for themselves. When they got to the spot where Morrison had sighted his "spectre," they found a black cow with a white face browsing among the chinquepin bushes!"

Big 'Fraid' and Little 'Fraid'

It is evident from the interviews of WPA writer James Taylor Adams and others, that the people of the valleys and hills of southwest Virginia, although largely superstitious and wary of ghosts, never lost their senses of humor, and loved to tell a "good one" on one another. The following example came from an Adams' interview with Mrs. Dicy Adams of Big Laurel in 1940. It had been passed down from her grandparents.

"One time there was a man, and he had a little boy. And he'd send the little boy after the cows of an evening. And he would stay and stay and stay and stay. Wouldn't get the cows home till way after dark. The man would whoop the boy. But that didn't do any good. He would stay out just the same.

"One day he told the little boy that something would catch him some night if he didn't quit staying out that a-way. He asked him if he was afraid. The boy laughed and said he'd never seen a 'fraid.' That gave the old man the idea of how he would scare him. So he told him there was 'fraids,' and he bet him that he'd keep on laying out till one would get him some night.

"So the next evening they sent the little boy after the cows. Had to go a long ways, maybe a mile or so. After he had been gone a long time and it was getting dusk-dark, the man told his wife he was going to cure the little boy of staying out that a-way, and he pulled a bed sheet off the bed and took off up the road.

"The family had a pet monkey and it had been learned to do everything it seed anybody else do, so it pulled a white table cloth off of the table and took right after him. The man never looked back and didn't see the monkey following him. So he went on till he come to a briar patch, and he wrapped the sheet around him and hid in the briar patch.

"The monkey, it wrapped the table cloth around it and slipped right in behind him. He never noticed the monkey. It wasn't long till he heard the cows' bells a coming, and the boy whistlin' along behind them. He let the cows get by and just as the boy was right fernence where he set, he raised up and stepped out.

"'Hoomph!' the boy said, 'a 'fraid!' About this time the monkey stepped out, too. The boy laughed. 'Another 'fraid,' he said. 'Two 'fraids. A big 'fraid and a little 'fraid.'

"The old man looked around and seed the monkey standing there wrapped up in the table cloth, and thought it was a real ghost. He took right down the road just as hard as he could go. And the monkey took right after him, right at his heels every jump.

The man looked back and seed it was a coming and he run faster than ever, while the little boy clapped his hands and hollered just hard as he could: 'Run, big 'fraid, little 'fraid'll catch you!'

"And the man never tried to scare the boy with hants anymore!"

******

What's Good for the Goose . . .

St. Luke's Church, four miles east of Smithfield, has been described as an "ancient and beautiful Gothic edifice." It was built in 1632, and is the oldest brick Protestant church in America. According to local legend, inhabitants of the area during the Revolutionary War buried the county records and the vestry books in an old trunk when they heard of an intended raid by British troops under Colonel Banastre Tarleton. Unfortunately, after the war when the trunk was dug up, many of the records crumbled to pieces.

The church was not used and remained in neglect from 1830 until the 1890s when it was restored. There is reason enough to suspect a haunting story or two involving St. Luke's Church. For example, buried in the adjoining graveyard are the remains of many Civil War casualties, and there have been a few residents who claim they have heard moans and cries emanating from the plots late at night. The reports are largely unsubstantiated, however.

A tradition that has survived was told by Mrs. H. D. DeShiell, who wrote a book on the history of Smithfield. Exactly when this episode occurred is not known, although it probably dates to the 19th century when the church was in sad disrepair, virtually in ruins.

Nevertheless, it still offered a semblance of shelter on the storm-tossed night a horseback rider approached it. No sooner had he tied his horse and propped himself up against a wall in a dry corner of the church, when something in the graveyard caught his eye. He described it as a "white, fluttering" sensation. Whatever it was, blurred by the rain and diminished in the darkness, it appeared to be trying to escape an open grave site. Whatever it was, the rider had seen enough. He and his steed galloped away toward town at thoroughbred speed.

The mystery was solved soon afterward, however, with a logical explanation. Either the frightened rider, or someone else, came

back in the light of day to investigate. What they found was a rather large goose, which had fallen into the open grave and couldn't quite manage an escape on its own, thus explaining the frantic fluttering.

It wasn't long after this, however, that a second paranormal sighting occurred at old St. Lukes. In fact, there were repeated sightings of a "wispy white apparition," in the cemetery. With each appearance, the legend grew that a ghostly woman "floated" among the tombstones.
The rumors became so rampant that no one would venture near the graveyard at night.

No one, that is, except a skeptical Dr. "Sandy" Galt, a well known and respected surgeon of his day. A veteran of the Civil War, it was said he knew no fear. And so, when he, too, sought shelter from a storm in the abandoned church one night as he was riding home from Carrollton, he didn't give a second thought about the stories of the ghost.

And then "she" appeared. In a flash of lightning, he saw a "whitish figure" flitting among the tombstones. Curiosity, not fear, motivated him to get a closer look . . . and the myth was unmasked.

The "apparition" was, in reality, a deranged woman who delighted in dancing about the old church yard in the dark, dressed in a long flowing white gown!

******

The Walking Skull

The following is excerpted from a letter to the editor published in the July 27, 1739, issue of the Virginia Gazette.

The letter writer told of an incident which occurred when two men were digging a grave in a country church cemetery. One of

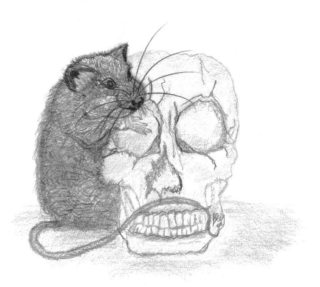

their shovels hit something solid. It was a human skull. They brushed the dirt off it and laid it beside the grave on some grass.

To their shock and disbelief, both men saw the skull moving on its own!

They raced to the little church and stammered what they had seen to the parson. He suspected the men may have been imbibing some alcohol while digging, but came out to see for himself. Sure enough, the skull moved. The wide-eyed parson shouted, "It's a miracle!"

He immediately sent for a cross and some holy water, and ordered the church bell to be rung. Curious parishioners flocked to the church. The skull was taken inside the building and laid on the altar . . . and there, the intrigue was quickly solved.

A tiny mole crawled out of one of the skull's eye sockets!

The gathered congregation members abruptly dispersed in all directions!

******

He'd Rather Have Seen a Ghost

The following interview with John Morgan Lipps was recorded at Wise, Virginia, by WPA writer James Taylor Adams on August 28, 1941.

"One time when I was a young man, I lived near Mendota. Old Peter Barker lived close there. Had a fine place and a fine house. He got to tellin' around that he was hearing something at his house. It kept on till he finally just give up and built a new house. Said he would rent me the house and farm for $25 a year if I would live in it. I don't believe in haints, so I took him up.

"So I moved in, and sure enough that night it started in. Went exactly like somebody slipping and crawling over the floor upstairs, or sometimes around the walls. I got up, looked everywhere, and couldn't find anything.

"But I noticed that when any of us made a noise that it would stop. So after I'd tried several nights to catch it, I decided to set up with it. We could hear it sometimes of a day, too, jes like somebody running their hand over the wall or ceiling. It did go ghostly all night.

"Well, I got me a flashlight and went upstairs where we heard it most, and set down and waited. After while I heard it start in, just slipping along like somebody in their sockfeet, slipping up on something. I waited til it had got going pretty good and was over right close to where I was setting. I'll admit I felt sort of shaky.

"But all at once I turned on my flashlight . . . and there, face to face, was the biggest black snake I'd ever seen in my life!"

******

The Cat that Purred from the Beyond

A half century or so ago near a small town a short distance across the western boundary line of Virginia, there lived an eccentric woman affectionately known as "Miss Effie." A spinster, she lived in a small frame house accompanied only by an old gray cat, unimaginatively named "Tom."

She took the feline everywhere, even to church services on Sunday mornings. This caused some consternation, especially to the local preacher, because when Miss Effie stroked Tom in her lap, the cat would purr loudly enough to disrupt the concentration of members during silent prayer ceremonies. Efforts to persuade Miss Effie to leave Tom at home proved futile. She countered that certain males in the congregation snored louder than her cherished pet purred.

Finally, at the ripe old age of 18, Tom passed on. This brought on a round of spirited speculation among the town's people. They all wondered if the grief-stricken Miss Effie would attend services the following Sunday. Consequently, the church was packed. Everyone sneaked glances toward where Miss Effie was seated. Then there were gasps. It appeared that she was stroking something invisible on her lap. The woman, they thought, had gone mad. Could she possibly think Tom was still alive? There was a stir of murmurs among the pews.

After a rousing sermon, the preacher called for a moment of silent prayer. It was then that everyone craned their necks, opened their eyes, and stared, with open mouths, toward Miss Effie.

As she continued to stroke, the distinct and unmistakable sound of a cat purring was heard throughout the building. It was so loud, some declared, that the church windows rattled!

******

The Mad Monks of Medmenham Abbey

(Author's note: The following did not occur in Virginia or anywhere near. It happened in England, but it is such a singularly rich and humorous anecdote that I couldn't resist sharing it. I found it in an obscure book at the Colonial Williamsburg Library: "Footnotes to World History," compiled by Harold S. Sharp.)

The Mad Monks of Medmenham Abbey were members of an unusual organization known as the Hell-Fire Club. It was founded by Sir Francis Dashwood in 1752, and included a number of Britain's "landed gentry." The purpose of the group was to satisfy desires for "a sexual establishment with its own clientele, apparel, and costumes." So Dashwood leased the 12th century Medmenham Abbey in the English countryside and had it renovated.

Club members met here periodically to indulge in obscene parodies of the Roman Catholic ritual. Satan was implored to appear and join the festivities. Sacrificial wine was drunk from human skulls, and women brought in for the occasions were dressed as nuns. In was a kind of farcical devil worship.

One participant in the irreverent merry making, John Wilkes, eventually became fed up with the "whole silly business," and decided to play a trick on the revelers. One night he dressed a baboon in a devil's mask and red suit, and hid him in a closet. When the wine was flowing freely and the merrymaking was going full blast that evening, and the carousers were entreating the "Evil One" to make an appearance, Wilkes opened the closet door and released the beast.

There was a desperately mad dash for the exit partaken by everyone except Lord Sandwich. He fainted dead away.

******

The Mystery of the 'Devil-Bat' Solved

Alexandria's venerable and historic City Hall building was designed in 1871. Practically as old is the enduring legend of a 'Devil-Bat' that, for decades, was thought to haunt the belfry. It apparently was an extremely elusive creature, for no actual sighting could be recalled by long-time residents, who nevertheless continued to pass along frightening stories of its existence. The case, however, was solved one day by a beloved town character named Louis Robert. His surprise finding was duly recorded by Eric Segal in his 1975 pamphlet, "Alexandria Ghosts."

Robert operated a framing shop in the market square area for many years, and one of his favorite pastimes seemed to be watching the crowds flow into town from the old North Boat, which, years ago, used to dock nearby and unload rowdy revelers, full of liquor, who "screamed, shouted, and generally raised hell" as they walked the streets in search of a rousing good time. One night a particularly rowdy mob decided for some reason that they would "tear down city hall." Robert left his shop and followed them to see what was going to happen. Fully aware of the legend, he mumbled to himself, "Devil-bat, devil-bat, keep this crowd back."

It was then that Robert said he thought he saw it. "I saw this big black thing zing around a corner, low to the ground, and stop at the doorway on the Royal Street side of City Hall." As the crowd got within a few feet of the entrance to the hall, Robert said, "just at the very last possible moment, this black thing shot out of the doorway like nobody's business.

"And then, well, the crowd just disappeared. In two seconds it was gone. Took off in all directions. It was real strange and I was scared, but I was curious, too. So I checked to see what it was and there, in the middle of the street, was the biggest darn skunk anybody ever saw!"

CHAPTER 6

A TREASURE TROVE OF
TOMBSTONE TOPICS

hen a person is dying, and knows he or she is not long for this world, they sometimes convey expressions of long suppressed feelings in their wills; feelings they were either too timid, too afraid, or too charitable to pass on while they were alive. Here are a couple of choice examples.

Telling It Like It Is

This will is excerpted from Williamsburg's Virginia Gazette, May

28, 1767. The author of it obviously had some strong opinions, especially about his ancestors, lawyers, the clergy, and women.

"I leave my body as a very wholesome feast to the worms inhabiting the vault of my family to whom I acknowledge myself extremely indebted for eating up my ancestors; particularly for their kindness in demolishing an old testy father, who left me at his death 50,000 pounds, although he was near about starving me during his life.

"To all practicing solicitors and attorneys I bequeath the following proverb, viz. 'Honesty is the best policy.' And this legacy I chose to give to those worthy gentlemen, it being the only one I can think of for which I can be sure they would not quarrel.

"To all unmarried women I bequeath cleanliness.

"To all coquettes I leave her a rotten reputation and the contempt of every man of sense.

"To all prudes, from my soul I bequeath virginity and wrinkles; or if they prefer having a bastard by their father's butler, groom or coachman, or any other butler, groom, etc., I desire my executors to give them their choice.

"To the Parson of my Parish and all other Parsons, I leave the following piece of advice; that they would not any longer expose their own weakness and absurdity by attempting to explain things which are mysteries, and consequently incomprehensible and above all explanation. . .

"To my three brothers, I leave my whole estate real and personal; to be divided equally among them; share and share alike, and my will is that if ever they marry, they should settle one farthing penny pin money to their wives!"

******

Present Company not Accepted

General Charles Lee served in the British Army in America in 1755. He was described as an eccentric bachelor who lived in a most peculiar house in Leetown, Jefferson County, Virginia, (now West Virginia.) It was deemed peculiar in that the divisions in the house, instead of being walls, were merely chalk marks.

Lee apparently did not like the colonists, in part because he was passed over for commander of the Continental Army when George Washington was appointed. This undoubtedly incensed Lee. In fact, once, when Washington was coming to Leetown, he sent word to Lee that he would like to dine with him the next day. Lee ignored the invitation, went hunting instead, and left a note on his door for Washington: "No meat served here today."

When he wrote his will, Lee added an unusual clause: "I desire most earnestly that I may not be buried in any church or church-yard, or within a mile of any Presbyterian or Anabaptist Meeting House, for since I have resided in this country, I have kept so much bad company when living, that I do not choose to continue it when dead!"

******

Retribution from the Grave

It is obvious from some wills of 200 or more years ago, that the departing patriarchs had distinct favorites among their heirs. Women, in particular, seemed to have been considered far less favorably than their male siblings.

In the 1734 will of Prince William County resident Michael Ashford, for instance, he left large tracts of land to his three sons, but "unto my daughters Ann, Mary and Constance, each of them one bed with the ruggs, blanketts and sheets belonging to them."

Thomas Simson, a carpenter in the same county who also died in 1734, apparently played favorites even among his daughters. To one, Mary Woodard, he left 100 acres of land. Yet to another, Ann Simson, he left "one cow and calf, one feather bed, rug, and two blankets" – and she was to get these only after her mother-in-law died!

When Elinor Sanders died, in Prince William County in 1739, she left her entire estate to her sister and her daughters – with this one exception: "unto my son, Hundley Elder, one shilling current money!"

One wonders what he did to deserve such treatment.

******

Old Time Funerals Could Be a Hoot

In Bruce's "Social Life of Virginia," the author notes that "More than a few Virginians (in the 17th and 18th centuries) requested in their wills that weapons and alcohol be omitted from their funerals in hopes of preventing 'excess'."

He explains that "a common part of the proceedings was a fusil-lade which, by the quantity of gunpowder, indicated the status of the deceased. Thomas Wall in 1650, in his will, requested 'three volleys of shot for the entertainment of those who came to bury him.' As many as ten pounds of black powder were expended on these occasions – enough for many volleys."

Such weapons, when mixed with alcohol, sometimes created a super-charged atmosphere.

Bruce: "At some funerals as many as 50 or 60 gallons of alcoholic beverages were drunk by a crowd of mourners who were highly volatile and heavily armed!"

******

How Not to Win Friends

The following obituary was printed in the Virginia Gazette on February 19, 1773:

"Departed this life, in the 50th year of his age, Thomas Low Thimble, after a series of bouts of drunkenness. It may be with truth be said, that no man ever died less regretted; the sound of his last trumpet gave a general joy to all his friends, as well as those who had the misfortune to be of his acquaintance. Take heed, ye sons of Bacchus, that when Death comes with his summons you may not be caught napping; as you see, was the case with Mr. Thimble!"

******

Don't Fence Us In

Master West Virginia storyteller Riley Wilson tells of the time he got a letter from a friend in Virginia asking him to contribute to an old family cemetery fund to build a fence around the graveyard.

He wrote back: "I don't think I care to contribute to a fence around a graveyard. You see, everybody that's outside doesn't want to get in, and those inside can't get out. So I don't reckon we need a fence."

******

An Ensemble of Enlivened Epitaphs

Tombstone inscriptions can sometimes be quite revealing as to the kind of lives the dearly departed led. Here are some classics.

Richard Cole, a wealthy planter from Westmoreland County, hopeful for turning over a new leaf in the afterlife, decreed that his stone include the following:

"Here lies Dick Cole, a grievous Sinner
That died a Little before Dinner
Yet hopes in Heaven to find a place
To Satiate his soul with Grace."
******

In a Suffolk cemetery, there is this whimsical note:
"Here lies poor Johnny Ford,
Who died from grog and not by sword
From cask to keg, he long did suck it -
He drank his fill, and kicked the bucket!"
******

Captain Archibald Willey's stone, near Ordinary, Virginia, puts things in perspective:
"A span is all that we can boast
     An inch or two of time,
Man is but vanity and dust
     In all his flower and prime."
******

In the Bruton Parish cemetery in Williamsburg, visitors may do a double take when they see this headstone:
"To the Memory of Mr. Charles Hunt late of this parish.
He died the 11th day of Oct 1794 Aged 41 years.
Regretted by all who knew him."
******

Old timers in Rockingham County say the following has been passed down for generations. Seems 150 years or so ago there was a horse trader who had the reputation of being a notorious liar. He allegedly had swindled a number of county citizens in his dealings. When he passed away, his family erected a tombstone inscribed in large letters with "AT REST."

Sometime later a man who the horse trader had once cheated went to the cemetery, and with a lumber pencil, added this to the inscription: "Here lies the Truth, AT REST, it never came out of him.!
******

In the hills and hollows of rural Virginia a century and more ago, formal schooling was scarce. Often children had to leave school at an early age to work on the farm, or to become an apprentice for a craft. For many, spelling wasn't a strong point. This tombstone inscription was found in an isolated graveyard in the far south-western part of the commonwealth:
"Gone to be an Angle."

******

In the early 1800s, Tom Fogg of Essex County, had a reputation as a wit and a native poet. One night after several drinks in a tavern, he was asked to write an epitaph for a friend of his named Keezel. He penned:

"There lived a man who died of late,
And angels for his coming did wait –
But in stepped the Devil like a weasel,
And down to Hell he took poor Keezel."

******

A husband's shortcomings were unveiled in this Williamsburg epitaph:

"Beneath this marble stone there lies
poor Tom, more merry much than wise;
Who liv'd for two great ends,
To spend his cash and love his friends.
His darling wife, of him bereft,
Is only griev'd – there's nothing left."

******

The following tombstone inscriptions spell long-sought relief for the grieving widowers:

Here snug in grave my wife doth lie,
Now she's at rest, and so am I!
I laid my wife beneath this stone
For her repose and for my own.

******

Here lies my wife in earthly mould,
Who, when she lived, naught did but scold;
Peace! wake her not! for now she's still:
She had, but now I have my will.

******

Here lies my dear wife,
A sad slattern and shrew,
If I said I regretted her,
I should lie too!

******

Somewhere in Surry County:
"In peaceful silence here we lie,
Back to back, my wife and I.
When Gabriel blows his horn so shrill,
If she gets up, then I lie still."

******

At Sherwood Forest, the home of John Tyler, the tenth President of the United States, there is a tombstone honoring his faithful steed.

"Here lieth the bones of my old horse, General, who served his master faithfully for twenty seven years, and never blundered but once – would that his master could say the same."

******

In an Alexandria cemetery, this tombstone reveals the multiple marriages of the deceased:

"An excellent husband was this Mr. Danner,
He lived in a thoroughly honorable manner,
 He may have had troubles
 But they burst like bubbles,
He's at peace now with Mary, Jane, Susan & Hannah."

******

On a tombstone in Thurmond, Maryland:
"Here lies an atheist. All dressed up and no place to go."

******

For some, death is a blessing. Consider the epitaph of Maximila Storer in Great Bridge Gardens:

"Affliction some 21 days I bore
Physicians were in vain
Till God above did hear my moan
And eased me of my pain."

******

And there is this gem on Margaret Daniels' stone at Hollywood Cemetery in Richmond:

"She always said her feet were killing her, but nobody believed her."

******

'TO HELL, MADAM!'

"Of all the strange epitaphs on tombstones in Virginia, one of the most quaint, curious and intriguing marks the burial site of John Custis, IV, on the Eastern Shore off state road 644 about four miles south of the town of Cheriton. Here, in the 17th century, stood a house called "Arlington," which was built by John Custis, II. It is notable for two reasons. It was to this plantation that Governor William Berkeley fled, in July 1676, during Bacon's Rebellion, after Bacon's forces had chased him out of Jamestown.

This also was where John Custis, IV, and his wife, Frances Parke Custis, lived – and fought! Their relationship was so tempestuous, in fact, that it became legendary. According to several book accounts, the couple constantly feuded. Custis, a wealthy land owner with a reputation as a "gay blade," and Frances, one of Virginia's most sought after belles, were married in Williamsburg in 1706.

The honeymoon didn't last very long, and perhaps for good cause. Custis has been described as being eccentric and irascible; Mrs. Custis as being "a Tartar, shrewish and curst." To put it succinctly, their marriage was a disaster. One author, perhaps charitably, said; "The alliance seems to have been a very unhappy one, and many stories of their contentious life have been handed down. Frances was a lady of much determination, which led to frequent conflicts with her eccentric husband."

The animosity grew so much that they would not speak to each other directly or use each other's name. Some accounts say such non-communication lasted for weeks at a time. One author, however, said they didn't speak to one another for 14 years! Conversation, when necessary, was done through their butler, Pompey. When they dined together, which they did do, seated at each end of a long table, Mrs. Custis would address Pompey: "Ask your master if he will have coffee or tea, with cream or sugar."

Custis' Tombstone

Custis would reply: "Tell our mistress that I will take coffee with sugar and cream." In addition, Mrs. Custis cordoned off the house. She took half and allowed her husband half, and she forbid him to enter her sanctum.

One day the silence was broken. Custis dressed himself with great care one morning, ordered his best horse and gig to the front door, and in the most polite and dignified manner, invited Mrs. Custis to accompany him on a drive. "Certainly," she responded. "Sir, I will be delighted, but when were you ever so courteous before?"

Instead of taking the usual route along the bay beach, Custis headed his horse straight out in the bay. "Where are you going, Mr. Custis?" Frances asked.

"To hell, Madam," he said.

"Drive on," she replied. "Any place is preferable to Arlington."

Presently, the water began to enter the gig. "Again, I ask where are you taking me to," Frances anxiously inquired.

"To hell, Madam, as I have already told you!"

"And again I say, drive on Mr. Custis. The prospect is far brighter than that of a return home," she retorted.

After proceeding so far out from shore that the horse was all but forced to swim, Custis turned the animal's head to the shore and said, with some emphasis, "If I were to drive to hell and the devil himself came out to meet us, I do not believe, Madam, that you would be frightened."

"Quite true, sir," she said. "I know you so well that I would not be afraid to go where you would go."

This bizarre incident apparently cleared the air enough to allow the couple to reach an agreement settling property differences. Even that document was weird enough to be worth noting. In it, Custis specified: "First, it is agreed that the said Frances shall return to the said John all the money, Plate and other things whatsoever that she hath taken from him or removed out of the house upon oath, and be obliged never to take away by herself or any other, anything of value from him again or dispose of anything of value out of the family without his consent . . .

"Second, that Frances shall henceforth cease to call him, ye said John, any vile names or give him any ill language . . . And that she shall not intermeddle with his affairs but that all business belonging to the husband's management shall be solely transacted by him . . .

"Neither shall he give her any but to live lovingly together and to behave themselves to each other as a good husband and wife should do . . .

"Provided also that the condition of this bond be that if the said Frances exceeds the allowance herein expressed in these articles, run him in debt or break any of them, the bond to be void and the allowance to cease . . ."

In the end, John Custis, IV, who survived his wife by seven years, had the final word. This is the epitaph he decreed for his tombstone, which is still visible today:

"Under this Marble Tomb lies ye Body
of the honorable John Custis Esqr.
. . . Aged 71 years, and yet lived but Seven Years which
was the space of time he kept a Bachelor's
house at Arlington on the Eastern Shore of Virginia."

******

Up or Down?

And finally there is this priceless anecdotal jewel that had faithfully been passed down, generation to generation, in the Shenandoah Valley for more than a century. It is said that a tramp, resting in a weed-covered graveyard, noticed the following epitaph:

"Remember me as you pass by
As you are now, so once was I
As I am now, so must you be
Prepare for death and follow me."

The tramp thought about this for some time, then added two more lines with some chalk:

"To follow you, I am not content
Until I know which way you went!"

C H A P T E R 7

HILARIOUS HAUNTS FROM THE HOLLOWS

s one effort to help get people back to work during the Great Depression, the U. S. Government, through the Works Progress Administration (WPA), commissioned a project whereby writers were hired to tour the nation and interview thousands of people on a variety of subjects. In Virginia, one part of this enormous endeavor was to collect, and hopefully preserve, colorful folklore – everything from home-grown remedies and cures, to back country recipes, to mountain ballads. Most of the interviews were recorded between 1937 and 1942.

Outstanding among this huge mass of historical data is the col-lection of James Taylor Adams, a prolific writer from Big Laurel, (Wise County), Virginia. Adams, in fact, had been accumulating such information even before the WPA work began, and he contin-ued long after it stopped. This collection alone, which includes the work of other writers, numbers in the thousands of pages.

Buried in the archive files of the Library of Virginia in Richmond, the Alderman Library at the University of Virginia in Charlottesville, and the Blue Ridge Institute at Ferrum College near Rocky Mount, are hundreds of such papers, from the Adams and other collections, relating to ghost lore.

Here, then, is a selection of some of the more entertaining entries, offered here through the courtesy of Clinch Valley College and the Blue Ridge Institute.

The Monster Ghost that Wasn't

The following is excerpted from an interview made by WPA writer Susan Morton in Prince William County on June 28, 1937. She tells of a slave known as "Uncle Tom Primus," who lived on the "Chapman Plantation." When he was a boy, he worked at a place called "Beverley's Mill."

Sometime in the early 1850s, the Manassas Gap Railroad put in a line that ran directly adjacent to the mill. The track had to be built up through the gap so that it was on a level with the second floor of the mill.

The first day the train ran, the young slave heard a "terrible noise" approaching as he was working in the mill. He looked out the window and saw a strange "puffing monster" heading straight toward him.

Petrified, he instinctively leaped into a bin of meal, and "nearly suffocated before he was pulled out."

******

One Haint too Many

This account was told to James Taylor Adams on February 24, 1942, by James W. Hays, Jr., of St. Paul (Sandy Ridge), Virginia.

"They say this actually happened . . . I've heard father tell it many a time. Said there was a man who worked away from home and had to pass an old abandoned house after dark, and that every night as he passed, he would see something like a person wrapped in a sheet hanging on or leaning against one corner of the house.

"He told about it, and there was one feller who laughed at him and plainly told him he didn't believe it. So the feller said if he didn't believe it, for him to just pass there after dark the next night and see if he didn't see it. The other feller said all right, he'd do that very thing.

"Now this feller who'd been seeing the haint was a church member and he got to studying if the other feller didn't see something he'd accuse him of actual lying, and maybe have him throwed out of church. So thinking he might have imagined he'd seed something – it might have been the moon a shining against a white log – he decided he'd better do something to convince the other feller.

"So he took a bed sheet and went to the house just after dark and wrapped the sheet around him and stood up against the other corner of the house from where he'd seed the booger. He couldn't bring himself to stand there where he'd seed the thing.

"So after awhile he heard somebody coming up the road a walking. Sure enough, it was the man who was passing to see the haint. Just as he got in front of the house, he stopped and looked and said, 'Well, I be confound, if they ain't a haint. Yes, by golly, there's two of them,' and he started to run.

"The man with the sheet looked across to the other corner and there was the thing he'd been seeing, and he throwed down his sheet and he run, too!"

******

A Scary Ride at Night

James Taylor Adams interviewed Robert Hammond, Tacoma, Virginia, on October 2, 1941. Hammond said he had heard this from his father, 50 years earlier.

"I've heard my father, Henderson Hammond, tell about an ole haunted house in Scott County. Nobody could live thar or even stay all night. They was a sort of a brave feller in the neighborhood named Hammond, some of our kinfolks. Well, sir, him and some other young men got together one day and agreed to go and stay in the haunted house that night.

"They met up and went long after dark awhile. Had to cross a high fence jes before they got thar. They all clumb upon the fence and was setting thar. All at once Hammond jumped off and they next thing they knowed they seed sumpin' jump up and him a straddle of its back, and kerstreak, it went away off across a field. They jumped off the other side of the fence and liked to killed theirselves a runnin' til they got home.

"Next morning they went over the Hammond's place to see if they could hear anything about him. He was there and told them he had jumped off the fence right smack a straddle of a cow's back and he thought it was the haint a running off with him til he happened to notice its horns, then he knowed it was a cow."

******

The Devil Dog that Defied the Drinkers

Among the superstitious-minded, reclusive residents of the hollows and hills of southwest Virginia in the 19th and early 20th centuries, there was a prevalent belief that animals, and especially dogs, sometimes "represented the Devil." Such was the case in this interview of Findlay Adams, recorded by James Taylor Adams in Big Laurel on May 12, 1941.

"One time, oh it's been 40 years ago I guess, Buck Gibson lived down there on Smoot Mountain. Si Adams and Rob Holcomb got together and made up their minds to go and get some liquor and go down to Buck's and get him drunk and have a big time.

"So they kotch their nags and pulled out right up the head of Smoot, going through by Sandlick Gap. Si told me about it. He said they was going riding along, the path jes wide enough for one hoss. Rob was in front and they'd got right up there above Pole Cat Hollow when all at once Si seed Rob's hoss rare up on his hind feet. And he heard Rob holler out sumpin.'

"He looked and jes ahead of 'em, there right in the middle of the path was the awfullest looking thing he'd ever seed. Big as a hoss. Hit was sitting back on hits hind parts in the road, and hit's eyes was as big as plates and shone jes like fire. His hoss seed it too and began to rare and pitch. Rob's hoss wouldn't go another step.

"So there they was; they tried to go round hit, but the hosses wouldn't go. The thing opened hits mouth and Si said he could see down hits throat. And it looked like a roarin' furnace of fire! They decided it was the devil and that hit was there to turn 'em back from going after liquor. So they jes turned around and went back home and left hit settin' there in the road."

******

The Dog that Broke a Man's Toe

Findlay Adams also told this to James Taylor Adams, on May 7, 1941:

"Talking 'bout ghost dogs, I guess you're heard about the dog ole Si Collins seed. One night Si was out in the yard between the house and kitchen and he noticed the kitchen door was a-standing open and he looked in and seed a big black, shaggy-haired dog standing in there by the table. Strange dog to him. He scolded him, but he never let on. Never moved. He scolded him several times, but he didn't pay no attention. He ventured in. He spoke to the dog and tried to march him out, but he wouldn't move.

"Si got mad. He drawed back and kicked at him. He foot went right on through (the dog) and struck the table leg and broke his big toe. I seed it. He couldn't wear a shoe for a month or two and hobbled around on a cane with his big toe all swelled up and turned blue.

"But after he broke his toe he run out of the kitchen and hollered for Aunt Paggy to fetch a light. She brought a light and they searched all over the place and couldn't find hair nor hide of any dog. He believed as long as he lived that it was the Devil he seed like a dog."

******

The Posthumous Ordeal of 'Old Dry Frye'

This is one of the classic legends drawn from the files of the Virginia WPA writers. It has been a favorite of story tellers for generations. It is an account, believed to be true, that occurred more than 100 years ago, and is based on an interview by Richard Chase in Proffit, Virginia, on April 10, 1942. The person interviewed was not named.

"Old Dry Frye was a preacher. Not much of one. Preached for his health, I reckon, and what chicken he could get. Anyway, he'd been going down to where a man named Johnny Martin lived at. Martin had a pretty wife, fairly young, and Old Dry Frye, he would go there when Johnny wasn't at home. But one Saturday night he miscalculated; went down to Johnny Martin's house, and Johnny WAS at home!

"Johnny was pretty mean, and he didn't care about knockin' folks in the head. So when Old Dry Frye knocked on the door and poked his head in the house, Johnny Martin come down with a stick of stove wood – Whap! Hit him harder than he aimed to. Killed him!

"'Law me,' he says. 'Now what'll I do?'

"So Johnny figured a while, then he took Old Dry Frye down the road a piece and stood him up at another man's door and went on back home and got in bed. And pretty soon, when that man had to go out after a turn of wood, he opened the door and in fell Old Dry Frye. That man's old lady liked to have throwed a fit, it scared her so, but he wasn't scared much. He just studied a while. He knowed where Old Dry Frye had had a habit of going, so he took him right back and stood him up at Johnny Martin's door, and knocked, and pulled on back home.

"Johnny Martin was scared to get up and answer, but directly he put on his britches and finally he went on and opened the door, and when Old Dry Frye fell back in the house, Johnny Martin says, 'O law! He's come back to ghost me!'

"Well the next morning was meeting day at the church and Old Dry Frye was due to preach that Sunday, so Johnny Martin decided what he would do. Way along in the night he took Old Dry

Frye up to the church house and throwed him down at the edge of the pool – big baptizing pool they had in that church, deep one too. And then he set a chair right close and gathered up Old Dry Frye and set him in it. Put his elbows on his knees and stuck his hands up under his chin, propped him up that-a-way. Then Johnny Martin, he went on home and slept sound.

"Next morning a boy come to the church house pretty early to make up the fires. He seen Old Dry Frye a setting there and says, 'Howdy, Mr. Frye.' Old Dry Frye never spoke. The boy come a little closer and says, 'Howdy, Mr. Frye.' Old Dry Frye set right on. The boy come right up to the edge of the pool and says, 'I said howdy Mr. Dry Frye.' Dry Frye never answered yet. That boy, now, he was a feisty young 'un, he didn't care how he spoke to nobody. He says, 'Look-a-here, Old Dry Frye, if you don't say howdy back to me, I'll knock your elbows out from under you!'

"Well, when the old man still wouldn't speak, that feisty boy reached over and knocked him a lick and over in the pool Old Dry Frye went, sunk right on to the bottom and clean out of sight! That boy thought he'd drowned the old preacher sure, and he was scared to death. But he couldn't do nothin' about it right then 'cause it was getting close to church time, and a few folks had started gathering and he hadn't built his fires yet. So he went to making up fires and didn't let on like nothin' had happened.

"And the folks all gathered and waited for Old Dry Frye to come and preach, and he never came, and nobody knowed where he was at. That boy would let out a giggle where he was settin' on the back row and the other boys would ask him what he was laughing at, and he'd just get tickled again and not tell 'em nothing.

"So finally they just sung a few hymns and took up a collection and got up to leave. Johnny Martin was there and he sung as loud as anybody else, and that Sunday, instead of a five-cent piece like he always done, he put a half dollar in the plate. And after the meeting broke and everybody went on off, that boy, he locked up the church and went on home to dinner.

"Then, 'way along late that night, he went and unlocked the church and got the old preacher out and put him in a sack, got his shoulder under it, and started slipping off to hide him somewheres. The moon was shining pretty bright by the time he got off a ways, and he crossed over a fence directly and went up a hill through an old field, a-stumblin' along under that sack.

"Now there was two men coming down on the far side of the

field right then, had 'em a sack apiece on their backs. The boy never seen them, but they saw him, and time they did, they both dropped their sacks and run lickety-split back over the ridge of that hill. The boy kept on up the hill, come across them other sacks directly, and he throwed his sack down, went and looked in the other ones. It was two big dressed hogs them two fellers had stole. So that boy drug his sack over there and left it, picked up one of the hogs and took it on back home.

"So the two hog-stealin' men looked back over the ridge directly, seen the two sacks a-laying there, and the one-sack boy gone, and they come on down, picked up the two sacks and went on home. They went to the smokehouse and hung their sacks up. It was dark, you know, and they couldn't see very well what they were doing.

"Next morning, the old woman got up to cook their breakfast, went out to the smokehouse to cut some meat. She reached up with her knife – and there hung Old Dry Frye! She hollered and dropped her butcher knife, and got away from there in such a hurry that she tore down one whole side of the smokehouse, broke off half the back porch, and knocked the kitchen door clean off the hinges! She was sorty scared.

"She hollered and yelled and told them men there was a dead preacher man hanging in the smokehouse in place of a hog. The men came running out in their shirt-tails and looked, seen Old Dry Frye hanging up there by his heels, and one of 'em says 'I thought that my sack was awful light coming in last night, and that hog's hide did feel sorty funny when I hung it up in the dark.'

"Well, just a day or two 'fore that, they had rounded up some wild horses that run out in the mountains around that place, so they went and picked out the wildest one in the lot, put an old wore-out saddle and bridle on it, and stuck Old Dry Frye on. Tied his feet underneath, tied his hands to the front of the saddle and pulled the reins through. Then they slipped out and opened the gate and let the horse go.

"Down the road he flew, with the old preacher on his back a-bouncing and tossing every whichaway, and them men run out and went to shooting and hollering, 'Stop him younder! He's stole our horse! Somebody stop him!'

"Everybody come out in the road a-shouting and a-hollering and shooting around, but the horse went so fast he was gone 'fore any-body could say scat. Took out up the mountain and right through the brush and in amongst the trees and up over the ridge and out of sight on the Kentucky side.

"And as far as I know, Old Dry Frye and that horse are over there yet,, a-tearing around through that wilderness!"

CHAPTER 8

CLASSIC CASES OF COINCIDENCE

oincidence: "the occurrence of events that happen at the same time by accident, but seem to have some connection." In the legends and lore of Virginia there have been some extraordinary instances where ghosts, or at least what were perceived as ghosts, made sudden and startling "appearances" at the most improbable moment. At times, this has caused not only stark fear to the witnesses, but instantaneously converted hard-core skeptics into life-long believers in the supernatural. Here are some cases in point.

'Miss Lizzie' Clears the Room

At the Victorian mansion, Edgewood, located on Route 5 in Charles City County halfway between Williamsburg and Richmond, owner Dot Boulware was entertaining a dinner table full of women guests one evening a few years ago. She was telling them about her resident ghost, "Miss Lizzie," who, since losing her lover in the Civil War, has occasionally "reappeared" at an upstairs window in apparitional form, with candle in hand, still hoping for his return.

Many people have claimed to have seen her, and others have heard or felt her presence in the house. One of Dot's guests, however, was having none of it. She said she didn't believe in such things and anyone who did was crazy.

Whether by coincidence or by psychic manifestation, at that precise instant, a heavy brass plate that had been atop a cabinet, suddenly fell off and bonked the woman squarely on the head.

Edgewood

Dot says that everyone sat in stunned silence for a second or two as the startling event soaked in. And then everyone got up in unison and rushed out of the room in such a hurry that several chairs were toppled.

******

The Man Who Sat Up in His Coffin

In Dickenson County, northeast of Big Stone Gap in the far southwestern tip of Virginia, Herbert Maynor Sutherland is somewhat of a legend. Born in 1893, he spent a lifetime recording oral histories of the hill men and women of that area of Appalachia called the Appalachian Plateau. One of the favorite traditions in his book, "Tall Tales of the Devil's Apron," was about a man known as "Hongry Jim Maggard."

Jim, in his sunset years, became virtually doubled up with rheumatism, and died when he was close to 90 years old. There were no undertakers nearby, so a friend, "Brandy Bill," built a home-made coffin. But when he and another friend, "Good Lige," tried to fit Jim in it, they had a problem. Because of his advanced condition, every time they pushed Jim's head down, his feet would fly up, and vice versa. Finally, they laid him out on a board and strapped his feet to one end and his head to the other.

A wake was held and friends and relatives gathered in Jim's house. Well past midnight, everyone left except Brandy Bill and Good Lige. The wind howled outside and caused the one lamp in the room to flicker. Hoot owls were hooting and an old dog was moaning "in a way that'd make a feller's ha'r stand up." Sutherland wrote: "Ye know, houn's allus seem to know when somebody's dead a'roun' the place, an' they howl ontel the cold shivvers run plum down yore back."

At about two in the morning, a big black cat slunk in through the open door and jumped up on the coffin. "It turned loose the most Gawd-awful howl ye ever heered," Brandy Bill said, "and I see Good Lige go over backards in his cheer. We jest set thar, us not a-bein' able to move bekaze we was too bad skeered. Jes about then thar was a noise of some sort over thar at the coffin an' we looked a-roun' to see whut it was. That strop that helt down Hongry Jim must a-broke bekaze the corpse riz right up in that coffin, an' Brandy Bill jumped like somebody'd stuck him with a pitch-fork!

"He grabbed that cat by the nap of the neck, an', on his way to the door, he stopped for a secon' er two at the coffin. 'Now, Hongry Jim, lay back down,' he says. 'Don' ye worry about nothin'. I'll put the cat out.'

"Then he went through that door like he was shot outta a gun, an' he never thought to drap that cat ontel he got plum home ag'in!"

******

A Ghostly Smack in the Face

Historic Fort Monroe, near Hampton, just has to be the most haunted military base in the world. There have been, over the past 170 years or so, scores of reports of spirits that seem to roam about freely – and many of them are famous! Apparitional sightings have included Abraham Lincoln, Jefferson Davis and his wife, Varina, the Marquis de Lafayette, Ulysses S. Grant, Indian Chief Black Hawk, and a budding young author named Edgar Allan Poe.

There are numerous nameless specters, too, including illicit lovers, and a bevy of perky poltergeists who, with unseen hands, playfully toss objects around. It may have been one of these that squelched an overbearing officer husband at the fort one night. He had a reputation for berating and humiliating his wife back in the days when such traits were often overlooked, or tolerated.

On this particular evening, he was in the kitchen and shouted some obscenity at his wife for some minor impropriety – perhaps she had left some dirty dishes in the sink – when, suddenly, a wet dish rag sailed across the room and smacked him soundly in the face!

He fell back a step or two, cursed, and then screamed at his wife, asking her if she had lost her mind. There was no reply. He looked around. There was no one else in the house. He found his wife out in the front yard, watering the lawn!

******

Never Insult a Ghost

Sherwood Forest, on Route 5, between Richmond and Williamsburg, was the home of John Tyler, tenth President of the United States. His grandson, Harrison Tyler and his wife, Payne, now live at this beautiful plantation site.

The ghost here is called "The Gray Lady," and is believed to have been a 19th century nanny. Apparently a child in her care died in the house sometime in the mid-19th century, and the spirit of the woman returns to rock the baby in a rocking chair. The Tylers and a number of friends and guests have seen the chair rocking by itself, and also witnessed several other unexplained manifestations.

Payne Tyler said she had finally had enough, and sat down one day in the parlor to have a talk with the ghost. She said out loud, "Look, you may have lived here at one time. I live here now. We are going to have to learn how to peacefully co-exist." Payne says the strange phenomena noticeably died down after that.

Sometime later Payne was in the house telling her cousin about the chat. The woman looked queerly at Payne, laughed, and said something like she thought Payne had more intelligence than that. It was ridiculous.

"Just then," recalls Payne, "the most amazing thing happened. The room we were in, the Gray Room, began vibrating wildly. A harsh downdraft of icy cold air seemed to pervade the room, and there were loud bangs, like shutters slamming against the house, although there was no wind to speak of. It was a most eerie feeling."

Payne said her cousin hurriedly departed, and didn't return to Sherwood Forest for several years!

******

Aunt Pratt Strikes Again!

Historic Shirley Plantation, a few miles west of Sherwood Forest, also in Charles City County, is the ancestral home of the Carter family; members of which have lived here continuously for nine or ten generations. Overlooking the James River, it is one of the most beautiful plantation mansions in Virginia.

It is open to the public, and visitors, upon entering a downstairs room, get a view of a large portrait of a woman, known as "Aunt Pratt," who can best be described as, well, homely. It is believed that she was Martha Hill, a family member who died in England in 1752. According to one account, the portrait, some years ago, was taken down from the front room and placed in an upstairs bedroom.

A distant relative came to visit and was given that room. After several restless nights, she complained that Aunt Pratt's "gaze" followed her around in the room, causing her great stress. So she finally confronted the painting, and as she did, she heard "someone moaning," and an arm chair began to rock with no one in it.

On another occasion some art experts came to Shirley to inspect the portrait. They found that Aunt Pratt had actually been painted over the earlier image of another woman. A psychic told the Carters that this woman's name was Cynthia. Subsequent research revealed that indeed there was a Cynthia in the family tree.

Then, two so-called "ghost hunters" came to investigate. When they entered the room where Aunt Pratt hung, chandelier lights flickered off. When they left the room the lights came back on. One said she felt "the strong presence of a woman in the room, but for some reason she didn't want to communicate with us."

When a new generation of the Carter family moved into the house a few decades ago, they decided to remove the portrait from its prominent position in a front room downstairs. They unceremoniously took it down and stored it in the attic. Aunt Pratt soon made her displeasure known to all. That night, and for some time afterward, strange noises were heard in the attic. It sounded like furniture being bumped around, and a woman crying. Searches found nothing to explain the cause. Finally, it was decided that Aunt Pratt was not happy where she was, so she was brought back to her proper place downstairs. Once this was done, the mysterious noises in the attic ceased.

In 1971, the portrait was loaned to the Virginia travel office for an exhibition on psychic phenomena in New York City. (State officials had heard of Aunt Pratt's shenanigans.) But, once there, she again expressed her unhappiness, in a most extraordinary manner. One morning the exhibitors found her off the wall where she had been placed, on the floor, and, in their words, "headed toward the exit!"

So, for security reasons, they locked the portrait in a closet at night. The sounds of a woman sobbing were heard through the door, yet no mortal being was inside. And one day the portrait had somehow escaped the closet and was again halfway to the exit. Once the exhibition was over and Aunt Pratt was returned to Shirley, the manifestations stopped.

Things then were quiet for the next 30 years. Then one day, as an historical interpreter was telling the story of Aunt Pratt to a group of tourists in the room which Aunt Pratt oversaw, a most bizarre thing happened.

A man standing in front of a large armoire sitting beneath the portrait, scoffed, calling the legends of Aunt Pratt a bunch of baloney. According the interpreter and other eye witnesses, just as he spoke, the doors of the armoire suddenly sprang open and banged him smartly on his backside.

And the room emptied in ten seconds flat!

******

Aunt Pratt

The Opossum that Caused a Panic

If it was just sheer coincidence, you could have fooled everyone who witnessed it. It was said to have occurred long years ago in the small town of Paris, southeast of Berryville. There was an old gentleman there who had told friends and neighbors that when he departed this world he would return in the form of an opossum. This, of course, invariably brought chuckles.

Some time later he died during a summer. As was the custom then, he was laid out peacefully on his bed, and relatives and acquaintances came over for the ritual of "sitting up with the dead."

The food and the conversation were virtually depleted around midnight, when the silence was broken by a loud scratching noise. Everyone in the room looked up. There, near an open, unscreened window, sat what was described as a "big, fat opossum" on the headboard of the old man's bed!

It goes without saying that the guests departed abruptly!

DIVINATIONS OF THE DEVIL IN THE OLD DOMINION

rom the earliest days of the first settlers in Virginia, and for centuries afterward, there was a fairly widespread belief, especially among the poorly educated, in the existence of the Devil. For many, such superstitious traditions had been carried to Virginia from the "old countries." Even King James of England, in 1597 – 10 years before Jamestown was settled – wrote that the Devil was present "Where (he) finds greatest ignorance and barbarity." He added that the abuses of witchcraft, derived directly from Satan, were "most common in . . .wild partes of the world."

If the king thought this, one can only imagine what the colonists must have wondered when they landed in Virginia in 1607, only to be greeted by the wildest looking, most bizarre acting people they had ever encountered – the native Indians! It must have seemed to the Englishmen that they had found the Devil incarnate!

In fact, these colonists deemed Virginia as the "favorite dwelling place of Evil," and as a battleground for the "forces of Light and Darkness." Captain John Smith referred to the Indians as "Devils," both because of their appearance and their "diabolical ways." He wrote that when he was captured once by the Indians, "They entertained him with the most strange and fearful Conjurations; As if neare led to hell, Amongst the Devills to dwell."

Colonist William Crashaw wrote, "Satan visibly and palpably raignes there, (Virginia) more than in any other known place in the world." Such beliefs, combined with the hostile attacks of the Indians, caused great fear at Jamestown Island, and later throughout the commonwealth. Especially feared were Indian chiefs and priests, the idols they worshiped and the ceremonial rites they held. The idols were described as being "inanimate representations of the Devil."

Coincidence, too, may have played a part in furthering the notion that the native Americans were in league with Satan. For example, colonist Alexander Whitaker and a group of men, exploring up the Nansemond River, came upon some Indians performing a wild dance the Englishmen had not seen before. An Indian told Whitaker there would be "very much raine presently." And, within minutes, a storm struck the area with "exceeding thunder and lightenings and much raine." It was enough to convince Whitaker. He wrote, "All which things make me think that there be great witches amongst them and they (are) very familiar with the divill."

So it should be of little surprise that the pioneering settlers who moved across the mountains westward perpetuated such beliefs. Many were thoroughly convinced that such an entity as the devil really existed, and this was passed on, generation to generation. Everything from failed crops to sick livestock was blamed on Lucifer, especially after some moonshine had been consumed. And some of the incidents involving this imagined evil were downright funny. Here are some examples.

******

The Devil Almost Got Him!

A young lady from southwest Virginia, who requested to remain anonymous, tells the following on her paternal grandfather. His mother, apparently, was a God-fearing, Bible-toting, no-nonsense woman who often told her son that if he misbehaved or disrespected her, "the Devil would come with a chain and drag him straight down to Hell!"

It happened that one night the grandfather, then a young man, stayed out late carousing with his friends. He had more than a snootful of home brew, and before he knew it, it was well past midnight. He knew he was in deep trouble. Finally, he started home. When he came to a point in the road where he had to pass between two fenced pastures, he heard the unmistakable sound of a rattling chain behind him. His heart nearly leaped out of his chest. He whirled around, but could see nothing in the black darkness. Then he heard hooves approaching.

In his inebriated state, he was certain the Devil himself was close on his trail. He started to run as fast as his legs would carry him. The sounds followed him – rattling chains, hooves pounding on the dirt road, and a low, inhuman moaning.

At last, he saw the farmhouse in the distance. As he got near it, he made out his mother standing, arms folded across her breast, on the front porch. Instead of screaming in indignation at him, she was laughing as hard as she could. He raced into her arms and begged for forgiveness, saying he would never again drink hard liquor or stay out late if she would only make the Devil chasing him go away.

He couldn't understand why she was so amused. Then he turned around the looked behind him. There was one of the family cows that had gotten loose and followed him home. Around its neck was a rattling chain!

******

'Satan' Offers An Unwanted Hand

Ninevah Jackson Willis, in her 1955 master's thesis on Carroll County folklore, tells the following, as collected from an old time resident.

"One time there was a graveyard down there before the woods was cleared out. Someone in the neighborhood died and they dug his grave. A footpath through the woods went right close to that new grave. It come night and the diggers went on home, aiming to come back against day and finish the vault.

"Well, funny thing, Old Man Press, he got drunk and was a-walking along that footpath towards home when he staggered off'n the way and fell smack dab in that grave. He was skeered to death, he fit, save his soul from Hell, and he hollered 'til he plumb gave out.

"Well, you know, Sam had been over to Ma's and she made a bed sheet for Sally, so he was a-taking it along home. It was sorta chilly, so he wropped it around him to keep out the night air. About that time he heard Old Press a-moaning down in that grave. he went, 'wait a minute and I'll come down there and get you.'

"Old Press looked up and saw that white sheet, give a yell you could have heard to China, and he took out up the side of that grave and didn't stop running 'til he got plumb home, a-yelling to his folks to lock the door; the Devil was after him!"

******

Reading the Bible in "The Flames of Torment"

WPA writer James Taylor Adams recorded this interview with Mrs. Lenore Kilgore of Big Laurel, Virginia, on February 26, 1941.

Mrs. Kilgore: "I've heard Uncle Sam tell the awfulest tale about old Ran Hubbard. He said old Ran lived on Critical Fork of Guesses River when he died. That's been 50 years or more ago. He had been a very wicked man, but on his death bed he was converted and requested that his Bible be buried with him.

"Now most of the neighbors objected to putting the Bible in the coffin with him, saying it was a sin to bury the Word of God. But old Ran had said bury it with him and here in this part of the country when a dying person makes a request it is carried out. So they finally placed it in his hands on his breast and buried him that way.

"Well, it went on for a few weeks, and Aunt Pop – that was Ran's wife – had a log rolling one day. Old Ran had cleared up a new ground before he died, but hadn't rolled the logs off of it. So all gathered in to roll the logs off of Aunt Pop's new ground. They had made one log heap right close to the house and that night after most of the people had gone, someone stepped out and come running back in the house pale as death and trembling all over.

"Said he'd seen something out there in the log heap that was burning in the yard. Uncle Sam said that him and Grandpa Roberts, who was Aunt Pop's brother, went out with some others who had stayed for supper and to talk a while, and sure enough, as plain as they ever seen anything in their life, there was old Ran Hubbard right there in the rolling flames with his Bible in his hands!

"They watched it for a long time and it was still there till they went to bed or went home. Everybody believed that it was a sign that old Ran had went to hell and was reading the Bible in the flames of torment!"

******

The Devil in the Steamer

The following anecdote is taken from the pages of the Confederate Veteran Magazine. It concerned a soldier, who, in dodging from a passing patrol during the Civil War, hid himself in a restaurant, by jumping into a large box used for steaming oysters. The lid closed with a spring lock.

"In a little while the colored man attending the apparatus turned on a full head of steam in order to prepare a mess of oysters for some customers. The soldier began to grow uncomfortably warm, and soon kicked and yelled lustily for liberation, until the frightened Negro ran away shouting that 'de debbil was in de steamer.'

"Other employees gathered around, hearing the noise, and released the perspiring soldier, who bounded with the speed of a machine whose motive power is steam."

******

A Stinging Funeral Oration

Folklore collector Elmer Smith, a former professor at Madison College in Harrisonburg, tells of the time, many decades ago, when a minister was conducting a grave side funeral service in Nelson County. He accidentally stepped on a nest of yellow jackets and they slowly crawled up his pant leg.

As he was saying, "The deceased was a grand man, he had the fear of the Lord in his heart," the yellow jackets began stinging, and the minister quickly added, "and I have hell and damnation in my pants!"

******

The Farmer's 'Curst' Wife

The following whimsical ditty, done to a chorus of "Fi di diddle i da diddle i diddle i da," was transcribed by Works Progress Administration writer Gertrude Blair in January 1942. Its origins are unknown, although it is obvious it was authored by a disgruntled and downtrodden husband.

"There was an old man owned a large farm,
And he had no horse to plow his land,
Then he hooked up the sow and the cow to the plow,
And turned the sod . . . the devil knows how.
The Devil come to the old man one day,
Says 'one of your family, I sure take away.'
Then said the old man, 'now surely I am done,
For the devil's done come for my oldest son.'
'It's not your oldest son I crave,
But your old scoldin' wife, I'll sure take away.'
'Then take her away with all your heart,
I hope from hell, she will never part.'
Then he shouldered her up all on his back,
And off he went, klinkerty clack.
Then he set her down at the forks of the road,
And he says, 'Old gal, you're a terrible load.'
Then he sets her down at old hell's gate,
And there he made the old gal walk straight.
Then two little devils come rattling their chains,
She off with her slipper and knocked out their brains.
Then one little devil went climbing the wall,
Says 'take her back daddy, she's murdering us all!'
Then he shouldered her up all on his back,
And like an old fool, he went luggin' her back.
The old man was peepin' through the crack,
And he saw the old devil come luggin' her back.
Then said the old man, 'we're bound for a curse,
For she's been to hell and she's ten times worse.'
The old man was laying sick in a bed,
And she took the butter-stick and paddled his head.
The old woman went, whistling over the hill,
Says 'the devil won't have me, I wonder who will.'
Then surely the women are worse than the men,
For they've been to hell and came back again!"

******

The Fiery Flames of Hell

George Tucker, the beloved columnist who wrote for Norfolk newspapers for many years, once told of an incident which occurred at Norfolk General Hospital many years ago. A man underwent a serious operation, during which a fire broke out in a pawn shop across the street. Following the surgery, the man, by chance, was wheeled into a room with a window facing the pawn shop.

As the anesthesia wore off and he opened his eyes, he was confronted by the flames from across the way. In his semi-conscious state he declared, "Lord have mercy! I knew all along that operation wouldn't be successful!"

******

The Devil in the Flour Barrel

(Author's note: This, I believe, is one of the true classic cases of ghostly humor. It took place more than 200 years ago in Amherst County, between Charlottesville and Lynchburg. It is based on an actual event and was recorded in a rare little booklet, "The Devil in the Old Dominion," written a half century ago by Alfred Percy, a masterful story teller.)

It involved an aging preacher named Aaron Crabtree. The year was 1802. Crabtree was in Amherst County, meeting with a wealthy planter named George Moreland, Sr., and his son, George, Jr. His purpose was to convince them to loan him ten acres of rich, creek-bottom land in a virgin forest for a camp meeting ground. Fervent religious revivals, with thunderous declarations of beating back the devil by emotionally-charged ministers of the day, were the rage of that era. Crabtree could envision himself saving thousands of backwoods sinners at an open tent gathering. People could come to such a glorious campground from the mountains and valleys for miles around. He had his heart set on such a driven mission.

He was, however, politely, but forcefully, turned down by the Morelands. Crabtree was disheartened, but he was not a man to give up easily. One fine spring evening he approached a tavern on a little ridge where the east-west road crossed the north-south route. What a wonderful site for a chapel, he thought.

The parson was welcomed into the tavern by a burly, stout inn keeper named Ira Beaton.

When Crabtree mentioned the area would make a good place for a little church, Beaton bristled, saying the folks hereabouts weren't very religious, plus it would be bad for his business. Beaton then rode off on an overnight trip.

At this point, a beautiful young girl came out to greet the preacher. She was Millie Beaton, Ira's wife. Crabtree raised his eyebrows. She was only about 20 years old, and Ira had to be more than twice her age.

The tavern was full with travelers and local farmers. It was Saturday night. As the evening progressed, the crowd became rowdy. Drinks flowed from the bar. After a while, the planter, George Moreland, and his son arrived. Crabtree, sitting quietly in a corner, observing, suddenly leaped up on the bar counter and began preaching.

"Watch out for the fires of hell that will be your lot if you don't recognize the Lord Jehovah and repent of your sins," he shouted. A stunned silence fell across the tavern as the imbibers looked up in astonishment. "Your time shall come and you shall face the forks in the road. One way leads upward to Glory and the other into the fiery pit," Crabtree bellowed. "Which fork will you take? Why the one to the pit with the molten brimstone to burn your lights and livers because you have no church to point out to you that better road of life; no vicar of God to show you the error of your ways. The noise I hear outside of this building now is the flapping of the devil's wings as he hovers peeping in the window."

Despite heckling from some drunken men, Crabtree, undaunted, stormed on. "Sinners such as you are fit fuel for the fire. You need prayer. You need a chapel where you can meet to worship." Glaring directly at the Morelands, he continued. "You need a camp meeting in the grove down by the creek where thousands may meet with you to ask for forgiveness of sin. You must have it for I see among you are those on the verge of hell. I see in their eyes, shame. I know of the sin that is in their hearts. Repent!"

Crabtree thought he might be getting through to just a few in the crowd, but just then a group of young people arrived for a square dance scheduled that evening. Fiddles and banjos appeared, hands began clapping, and the impromptu sermon was unceremoniously and abruptly halted.

The chagrined preacher, unnoticed by the merry makers, slipped down off the bar and retreated into the vacant parlor which adjoined the tap room. There was a sofa, a deep chair, and a flour barrel off in the corner of the room. Crabtree, exhausted from his never-ending battle against Satan, sank down into the chair, deep in meditation.

Sometime later, with the noisy dancing continuing, he heard the sound of the door opening. The shadowy figures of a man and a woman quietly entered and sat down on the sofa. They were totally unaware of the preacher's presence on the other side of the darkened room.

It was George Moreland, Jr., and Millie Beaton, the inn keeper's young wife. Crabtree couldn't help overhearing their whispered talk. Moreland was pleading with Millie for her to leave Ira and run away with him. She asked for him to be patient, that Ira would go on an extended trip in a few days and that would give them the opportunity to leave. They embraced and kissed.

Just then the music in the other room stopped, and Crabtree and the couple heard the revelers greeting Ira Beaton! His meeting had been cancelled and he had arrived back at the tavern totally unexpected. Moreland and Millie froze in fear. Thinking quickly, she told her lover to hide in the flour barrel, for Ira would surely enter the room in a minute or two to hang up his coat. Moreland did as he was told.

Crabtree then stood up, and Millie saw him for the first time. Then the door burst open and Ira entered. Millie rushed to her husband and greeted him. She told him she had been showing the parson the parlor.

Suddenly, a light flashed in Crabtree's mind. Maybe he could get his camp ground after all. He would hold the secret of the two lovers over young Moreland's father. He would threaten to expose the couple otherwise. He hated the thought of such blackmail, but he reasoned with himself that the Lord sometimes moved in strange ways.

Then, at the last instant, he had a change of heart. He couldn't go through with the ruse. He would have to expose the mortal sin he had just experienced with his own eyes and ears. His dream of the camp ground would be gone, but otherwise he wouldn't be able to live with himself.

As the mob from the other room pushed and shoved to get a view of what was going on in the parlor, Crabtree seized the moment. He told Ira that the room was full of sin, and to prove it he was going over to the flour barrel, where he said the devil himself was hiding.

He snatched off the lid. As author Percy wrote: "A ghastly, white, wild-eyed creature shot out of the barrel as though impelled by springs. The parson hadn't counted on this whited wraith of a human. However, he paused hardly a second before he shouted, 'Satan! Satan! The ghost of evil sin and shame!'"

As women screamed and fainted, and the men stood in awed disbelief, Moreland ran out of the room through the service door and disappeared into the kitchen. "For Gawd! It's a hant," declared a startled cook. One man, heavily fortified with drink, swore he saw the figure float through the kitchen, and glide past the back yard into the woods beyond, where "it" vanished. The stunned witnesses truly believed they had seen a real ghost.

Crabtree, taking full advantage of the situation, offered a prayer. Everyone prayed! Then the preacher thanked George Moreland, Sr., for lending ten acres of creek bottom land for a camp meeting ground. "It's the first step to keep that ghost from taking some human form we might all know," Crabtree said.

The visibly shaken, but quickly comprehending Moreland, not only agreed to lend the land, but offered ten additional acres as well.

Parson Crabtree smiled, looked upward, and said to himself, "Praise the Lord!"

PRICELESS HEIRLOOMS FROM THE PAST

 he best for last! Here are some masterpieces of ghostly mirth; magnum opuses of haunting humor. Enjoy!

A Scary Scene at Stonewall Cottage

The following account was contributed by J. B. Yount, a Waynesboro attorney, and is excerpted from the family history he wrote. Some of his relatives had a home called Stonewall Cottage on the valley turnpike just north of Harrisonburg. It was here that this incident took place.

"This occurred in 1934, when Aunt Laura died sitting up in her chair one night. She apparently had suffered a fatal attack during the evening, before coming upstairs to bed, and her body was not discovered until the next morning. Aunt Laura had left instructions that she wanted to be buried in a shroud. . .

"The undertaker had prepared the body in the coffin and placed it, as was the custom, in the front parlor. The house was dark, the shutters still closed in the front, seldom-used rooms. My father went around to the rear where the family and friends were gathered. After a while, Aunt Sallie asked my father to go over to the parlor to get her something from behind the organ. He had to pass through several rooms and the hall to get to the parlor.

"My father always said he wasn't afraid of anyone living, but he didn't like to fool with the dead. Nervously, he entered the parlor . . . he glanced at Aunt Laura, her eyes closed, her form lying stiffly in the coffin. He walked past to the end of the room and reached behind the organ.

"Suddenly, he heard a loud snap, which he always described as sounding like a rat trap going off. He looked around and saw Aunt Laura in the coffin, her eyes opened and apparently staring at him, her head turned in his direction, her false teeth half out of her opened mouth!

"My father claimed he was so much in shock that it took what seemed an hour for him to walk past the coffin and leave the parlor. He called out the front door to the undertaker, who came immediately.

"What had happened?

"Because of the delay in discovering the body, staying as it was in a sitting position all night long, rigor mortis had set in. The undertaker had braced her mouth shut with a brace under her chin, obscured by the high collar of the shroud. My father apparently jarred it loose as he walked across the creaky floor. The brace slipped, throwing the head ajar . . .

"My mother remembered well how white and pale he looked when the returned to the Stonewall Cottage kitchen."

******

Chicken and Dumplings for the Departed

Stephen Goens of Newport News tells of the following incident which he witnessed.

"A few years ago I went to an African-American church funeral service for a man named Brown whom I had known. The preacher was in the middle of his eulogy when, suddenly, a large woman appeared at the door and began walking down the aisle toward the casket, which was draped in flowers. The woman was carrying what appeared to be a large casserole dish, and even from where I sat, in the middle of a pew, you could smell a pungent odor wafting in the air.

"When she got close to the front, the preacher asked her what she was doing. 'I'm taking some chicken and dumplings to Mr. Brown,' she said.

"'You don't understand, sister,' the minister answered, 'Mr. Brown has gone on to his great reward.'

"The woman stopped in front of the coffin and said, 'It is Wednesday, isn't it?' The minister said, 'yes it is.'

"Well then, I have fixed chicken and dumplings for Mr. Brown every Wednesday for the past 30 years! The somewhat flustered minister said, 'that may be, but he can't eat it now.'

"To this, the woman huffed, with righteous indignation, 'if that's the case then, I guess Mr. Brown can smell the damn flowers!'

"She then placed the dish next to the bank of flowers and seated herself for the service."

******

The Corpse that Ate a Potato

Along similar lines, there is an old Negro folk tale, centered in Floyd County, Virginia, concerning the death of one of the elder members of a family that lived in a log cabin in a rural area. The deceased was in a coffin in the main room of the cabin. Members of the family were "sitting up with the dead." They had put some potatoes on the fire to roast, but, as it was late at night, they had fallen asleep.

By chance, two hunters came upon the little cabin, perhaps drawn by the smoke from the chimney. They peered through one of the windows, and, being famished, they quickly concocted a diabolical plan. They slipped into the cabin and stole the potatoes. Before they left, however, they set the head and shoulders of the dead man up in the coffin, pried his mouth open, and put one of the potatoes in it. Then they went outside and looked again through the window, waiting to see what happened when the others woke up.

The first one who awakened, stretched, then looked back toward the body. He then let out the most blood-curdling scream, and shouted, "Grandpa's done come to and eat up all the potatoes! There he sits with one in his mouth! He then lit out of the house as fast as his legs would carry him. The others, aroused, followed in close pursuit.

The last one out, however, caught his overall suspenders on the door latch, which had a hook on it. Fearing that he had been grabbed by the corpse, he fainted dead away. It was quite some time before any of the others went back to check on him.

******

The Woman Who Rose Up in Her Coffin

In the sleepy, pre-restoration days of Colonial Williamsburg – the late 1800s and early 1900s – one of the most enterprising merchants was a woman named Mrs. Braithwaite. Described in her youth as "one of Williamsburg's prettiest girls," she wore only black in her later years. Her large and full skirts were black, her blouses, with billowing sleeves, were black, and so were her low-heeled, laced, patent leather shoes.

At a site where the old printing shop now stands, on Duke of Gloucester Street, she ran three businesses; a dry goods store, a bicycle shop, and a funeral service. It was not a funeral home per se, for such places were not known in those days. Rather, coffins were made here, and horse and buggy-drawn hearses were rented. The actual services were conducted in the homes of the deceased.

Embalming then was still viewed by many with skepticism. More often the "old method" of using rubbing alcohol and ice packs placed against the corpse was preferred. In the funeral processions, horses were hitched to a black hearse for men; a white hearse for women and children.

A local carpenter named Johnnie Stover made the coffins. One day he had just finished one and went outside for a break. At the same time, a woman was telling Mrs. Braithwaite about a friend of hers who was on her death bed, and would soon need Mrs. Braithwaite's services. When the woman left, Mrs. Braithwaite, who figured she was about the same size as the dying woman, decided to crawl into the freshly made coffin to see if it would provide a proper fit.

As Stover reentered the building, he saw a white-haired old lady wearing a black blouse slowly pull herself up out of the new coffin. He grabbed his hat and dashed frantically out the front door.

It took Mrs. Braithwaite three full days to convince him to return to the shop!

******

The Man Who Rose Up from His Coffin

From the pen of V. N. (Bud) Phillips of Bristol comes this gem of
a true story that occurred toward the end of the Civil War.
Historian Phillips included it in his book, "Pioneers in Paradise."
Oliver Caswell King, a native of Holston Valley, near Bristol,
became a Confederate soldier and was severely wounded in a battle in northern Virginia. The nature of his injury was such that he
could not stand or sit without suffering unbearable pain. His only
relief, and slight at that, was to lie down completely prone.

After recuperating to an extent, he decided to try and go home.
To make the trip by train, he had a special coffin-like box made
with extra padding. He laid down flat in the box which was
placed in the baggage compartment along with several coffins containing the bodies of dead soldiers, all bound for Bristol.

When the train arrived at the depot some men started unloading
the coffins. The door of the baggage car was high, so the men had
to lift each box onto their shoulders before lowering it to the platform. Without looking into King's crate, they lifted it up and one
man said, "I wonder whose box this is?"

At this, King raised his head up, peered over the top of the box,
and said, "Why this is my box, Oliver Caswell King!"

As Phillips reported, the men instantly released the box and fled
in sheer terror. But when they dropped it, it tilted and slid downward, "dumping its hapless occupant onto the crowded depot platform." At the sight of this the crowd stampeded out of the train
station, and were last seen running far down the darkened streets
in all directions.

******

I'm Not Dead!

This is taken from the diary of Landon Carter, one of the sons of
Robert "King" Carter, one of Virginia's wealthiest land owners in
the early 18th century:

"Sam's boy, Johnny, died this day. A subject for much conversation . . . Had a grave dug for him, being laid out, but all at once
was discovered a groan, after some hours of stiffening . . .

"He ran away and hid (can you blame him?)"

******

Counting 'Walnut Souls'

The following is a time-honored legend which has been told and retold in southwest Virginia for generations. The exact date and location are unknown.

One evening two small boys stole some walnuts. On their way home, as darkness was upon them, they walked past a graveyard and decided to go in and divide up the spoils. They dropped two walnuts as they entered, but didn't stop to pick them up.

Then they went to the back and sat down behind some tombstones. One boy kept saying, "this one is mine, and this one is yours." Coincidentally, a deacon in a local church happened to pass by the cemetery at this time, and he heard the boys, but in the blackness, he couldn't see them. He heard, "you take this one, and that one is mine."

Terrified, the deacon dashed to the nearby church and told the preacher that he believed the Judgment Day was coming. When asked why, he replied, "because the Lord and the Devil are in the graveyard dividing out souls!" The preacher wasn't convinced, so the two men walked to the cemetery, and as they approached it, they heard, "this one is mine, that's yours. Now let's go get the two at the gate."

The preacher and the deacon departed the scene in great haste!

******

Hooded Visions Rise from the Mist

A few years ago, in the midst of a severe winter, tourism was way down in Williamsburg. So one day when five colonial historical interpreters were invited to visit an old church in neighboring New Kent County and learn of its history, they readily accepted. They were driven to the site, and because of the cold weather, they were wearing long hooded cloaks over their colonial costumes.

After the tour they came outside and sat down on a bench in front of the cemetery adjacent to the church to wait for their ride back to town. It was now nearing dark and it was drizzling slightly.

Pretty soon they heard a vehicle coming up the country road. Assuming it was their ride, these five women in their colonial costumes, with long cloaks and hoods . . . in the dusk . . . in the mist . . . arose in unison, with the shadowy tombstones in the background.

And it wasn't their ride! It was a tourist from New Jersey. The ladies said he took one look at them . . . and promptly drove into a tree! And never got out of his car to examine the damage!

******

The Civil War Soldier in the Cemetery

The following is told by Vincent Curtis of Chesapeake, who has been a member of the North-South Skirmish Association since 1954. The NSSA is an organization of reenactors who dress in authentic reproduction Civil War uniforms, and carry rifles, knapsacks, haversacks, and other accouterments. Curtis says that he became fast friends with two old time members, Jack Rawls and George Oswald.

"One weekend about 45 years ago, the 1st Virginia Volunteers were to attend a shooting match in Petersburg, and Jack and George decided to drive up there together. The two of them felt it would be easier and quicker to just dress in their Confederate uniforms and other equipment at home instead of changing at the shoot and again afterwards. After the shoot they got in their car and drove home to Norfolk.

"Now there is a large cemetery in Norfolk facing Granby Street, and Jack lived behind the cemetery facing the other street. When they got to Norfolk, Jack told George to let him out at the main entrance to the cemetery and he would walk home through it. That way George could turn around and drive home instead of driving around the cemetery which was a distance out of the way.

"Jack got out, put on his hat, knapsack, and haversack, put his rifle over his shoulder, and started to walk away through the cemetery. George then drove down to a place where he could turn around, and headed home. As he passed by the cemetery again, he saw a car had gone through the fence on the other side, knocked over a headstone, and was lying on its side. Since he was in a hurry and there were already some people gathered at the site, George didn't stop.

"A few weeks later at a luncheon, George met the manager of the cemetery and asked him about the wreck he had seen. The manager said it was a sailor, and they suspected he had been drinking, because he kept trying to tell them he had lost control of his car when he saw a Confederate soldier walking through the cemetery among the tombstones!"

******

'Don't Mess with Me, Ghost!'

In the April 19, 1875, issue of the Alexandria Gazette, there is this gem:

"The last sensation in Alexandria was a ghost. It flitted about in white garments and chalked up houses and fences in the most reckless manner. On being investigated with a rolling pin by a strong minded woman it endeavored to scare, the ghost proved to be an interesting widow with a taste for practical jokes.

"... She is now convalescing!"

******

The Appearance of the Devil – in Person!

Author, historian and folklorist Elzie "Sock" Mullins, a native of "The Pound" in the far reaches of southwestern Virginia, for years wrote a newspaper column called "Tales from South of the Mountain." In one of these, a classic, he tells of a rural school where teachers and students decided one year early in the 20th century, to hold a masquerade party for Halloween.

One seventh grader dressed in a bright red suit as the devil. On the appointed night, the lad started walking to the school, a mile or two away. Enroute, a storm came up suddenly. Seeking the nearest shelter, the boy saw the lights on in a little country church. He raced toward it.

Author Mullins described what transpired next: "It just so happened that in the church they were in the midst of an old time revival meeting. The preacher was reminding them that according to the Book of Revelation, that the end of time was near. He said, 'the Lord is going to soon call you or the devil is coming after you.'

"At that very instant, a loud crack of thunder and lightning sounded and the boy burst in the front door wearing his red devil outfit, horns on his head and pitchfork in his hands!

"Such screaming, you never heard before! The preacher made a mad dash for the back door. Out the windows some of them went like scared rats when a weasel invades their den.

"For pure mischief and excitement, the boy drew his pitchfork back in a menacing way and charged up the aisle. Within a minute, everyone had vacated the building except an old crippled man.

"He turned facing the boy, threw up both hands and nervously said, "I've been a member of this church congregation for over 30 years . . . but I've always been on your side!"

Author L.B. Taylor, Jr., and illustrator Brenda Goens.

About the Author

L. B. Taylor, Jr. – a Scorpio – is a native Virginian. He was born in Lynchburg and has a BS degree in journalism from Florida State University. He wrote about America's space programs for 16 years, for NASA and aerospace contractors, before moving to Williamsburg, Virginia, in 1974, as public affairs director for BASF Corporation. He retired in 1993. Taylor is the author of more than 300 national magazine articles and 35 non-fiction books. His research for the book "Haunted Houses," published by Simon and Schuster in 1983, stimulated his interest in area psychic phenomena and led to the publication of five regional ghost books preceding "The Ghosts of Virginia."

The author is available, depending upon his schedule, to speak on the subject of Virginia ghosts to civic, social, fraternal, business, school, library and other groups. Call or write with dates and details.

If you have a ghostly or unusual psychic encounter you would like to share with L. B. Taylor, Jr., for possible future publication, please call or write the author.

L. B. Taylor, Jr., 108 Elizabeth Meriwether, Williamsburg, VA 23185
Phone: (757) 253-2636 * Fax: (757) 253-9415
Web Site: www.vaghosts.com * Email: vaghost@rcn.com

The following books by L. B. Taylor, Jr., are available directly from the author:

"The Ghosts of Virginia, (Volume VIII)," (472 pages) $16

"The Ghosts of Virginia, (Volume VII)," (472 pages) $16

"The Ghosts of Virginia, (Volume VI)," (466 pages). $16

"The Ghosts of Virginia, (Volume V)," (480 pages) $16

"The Ghosts of Virginia, (Volume IV)," (473 pages). $16

"The Ghosts of Virginia, (Volume III)," (462 pages). $16

"The Ghosts of Virginia, (Volume II)," (407 pages) $15

"The Ghosts of Virginia, (Volume I)," (401 pages).. . . . . $15

"Civil War Ghosts of Virginia," (240 pages) $13

"The Ghosts of Williamsburg" (84 pages) $8

"The Ghosts of Williamsburg, Volume II," (194 pages). $13

"The Ghosts of Richmond" (172 pages) $12

"The Ghosts of Tidewater" (232 pages). $13

"The Ghosts of Fredericksburg" (192 pages) $12

"The Ghosts of Charlottesville and Lynchburg" (192 pages). . . $12

"A Treasury Of True Ghostly Humor" (126 Pages) $12

SPECIAL: All 8 Virginia books, a $126 value. $110

SPECIAL: All 16 books, a $221 value $200

Please add $3.00 for shipping on single book orders, $5.00 for multiple book orders, payable by check or money order. If you wish the books signed, please specify to whom.

OTHER BOOKS BY L. B. TAYLOR, JR.
PIECES OF EIGHT . . . . Recovering the Riches of a
. . . . Lost Spanish Treasure Fleet
THAT OTHERS MAY LIVE (Air Force Rescue & Recovery Service)
LIFTOFF: The Story of America's Spaceport